GREAT QUESTIONS OF CANADA
ESSAY COMPETITION

The Dominion Institute is offering an annual two-thousand-dollar cash prize for the best student essay on the eight topics explored in *Great Questions of Canada*. The winning entry will be published by the Dominion Institute online at www.greatquestions.com.

Full details on the essay competition and extensive online educational resources can be accessed at www.greatquestions.com. The competition is open to senior high school students and history and political-science undergraduates aged twenty-one and younger. The annual deadline for submissions is the second Monday in May. Each year's winner will be announced by the Dominion Institute on the second Monday in September.

The Great Questions of Canada program is an initiative of the Dominion Institute, a national charity founded in 1997 to promote better understanding of Canadian history and civics. The program was originally sponsored by Operation-Dialogue.com, Magna International, the Historica Foundation of Canada, and the *National Post*.

The Dominion Institute acknowledges the generous support of Key Porter Books for the *Great Questions of Canada* essay competition and for the reissue of this expanded publication.

GREAT
QUESTIONS
OF
CANADA

EDITED BY
RUDYARD GRIFFITHS

KEY PORTER  BOOKS

Library and Archives Canada Cataloguing in Publication

Great questions of Canada / Rudyard Griffiths, editor. — 2nd ed.

ISBN-13: 978-1-55263-861-3 ISBN-10: 1-55263-861-8

1. Canada.   2. Canada—Politics and government.   3. Canada—History.
4. Nationalism—Canada.   I. Griffiths, Rudyard

FC97.G73 2007   971   C2006-906413-X

The publisher gratefully acknowledges the support of the Canada Council for the Arts and the Ontario Arts Council for its publishing program. We acknowledge the support of the Government of Ontario through the Ontario Media Development Corporation's Ontario Book Initiative.

We acknowledge the financial support of the Government of Canada through the Book Publishing Industry Development Program (BPIDP) for our publishing activities.

Key Porter Books Limited
Six Adelaide Street East, Tenth Floor
Toronto, Ontario
Canada M5C 1H6

www.keyporter.com

Text design: Marijke Friesen
Electronic formatting: Jean Lightfoot Peters

Printed and bound in Canada

07 08 09 10 11 5 4 3 2 1

CONTENTS

ACKNOWLEDGEMENTS

Great Questions of Canada is the product of the efforts of a remark-able group of public-spirited individuals and corporate and government sponsors.

The early direction provided by Peter White, Ken Whyte, and Mel Hurtig was responsible for the initial appearance of these essays as a *National Post*/Dominion Institute editorial series. The energies of Michael A. Levine and Bruce Westwood were the all-important catalysts for the first edition of this book. Assistance along the way was provided by Adrienne Snow, Malcolm Jolley, Ashton Westwood, Erik Penz, and the Honourable Michael Chong. *Great Questions of Canada* would not have been possible without the vision and generous financial support of the Millennium Bureau of Canada and its minister the Honourable Herb Gray, Chapters bookstores, TD Bank, and Magna International.

The Dominion Institute wishes to give special thanks and its heartfelt appreciation to Key Porter Books for agreeing to reissue this book and for providing the necessary financial resources to engage four new authors to write on two compelling new topics.

Finally, the Dominion Institute would like to acknowledge the hard work and dedication of Pat Kennedy, who acted as the Institute's "in-house" editor on this project.

Great Questions of Canada is a project of the Dominion Institute, a national charity dedicated to the promotion of Canadian history and civics.

PREFACE TO THE SECOND EDITION

Great Questions of Canada was first published in 2000. The book grew of out of a major editorial series that the Dominion Institute and the *National Post* created to encourage debate, in the run-up to the second millennium, about the major challenges facing our country.

In this, its second and expanded incarnation, *Great Questions of Canada* provides readers with the opportunity to delve into the ideas, arguments and at times sharply contrasting points of view of the twelve authors who contributed to the original version. As a bonus, the Dominion Institute has commissioned four new essays on two topics that continue to shape the political and cultural landscape of our country: multiculturalism in a post-9/11 Canada and the fate of the country's aboriginal communities in a changing world.

As in the original edition, the new essays, undertaken by George Jonas and Haroon Siddiqui and by Jean Teillet and Tom Flanagan, provide readers with a set of very different vantage points on common issues of national concern. It is the hope of all of us involved with this project that, through the lively exchange of ideas, *Great Questions of Canada* will encourage not only better and more reasoned arguments in classrooms and around dining-room tables, but also, at the end of the day, the prospect for national conciliation and the development of solutions to the issues that will define our collective destiny.

—Rudyard Griffiths
Executive Director
The Dominion Institute
January 2007

INTRODUCTION

BY RUDYARD GRIFFITHS

CANADA'S CIVIC CULTURE has long been marked by a powerful interest in institutions and the programs they deliver as the embodiment of the values we share. Year after year, opinion polls reveal that medicare and social programs function as symbols of our collective sense of civic responsibility for one another. Our political debates studiously shy away from the discussion of first principles and founding concepts. Instead, we dwell on the ways parliamentary and government institutions succeed, or fail, in representing our collective will. On the world stage we excel in the intricate institutional arts of multilateral diplomacy, peacekeeping and humanitarian assistance. The dominant role institutions have played in fashioning both our distinctive way of life at home and the confidence with which we act intergovernmentally and through non-governmental organizations abroad—the case with which we institutionalize the values we share in common—is a hallmark of the Canadian identity.

But it was not always this way. Ideas once had a greater influence over the character and direction of Canada's civic culture. As Canadian institutions come under increasing stress, as the authority of institutions wanes in a world of value change and globalization, we need to return to founding concepts and to democratic debate about governing ideas that can help us realize our full potential as a community.

Think of the heady mix of issues and ideas, the political zeitgeist that animated the country at the time of Confederation. Looking back fourteen decades, it is hard to imagine how a balancing act as intricate as federal union was achieved out of the colonial culture of the 1860s. Canada at Confederation was a patchwork of colonies each divided along fault lines of language, religion and ethnicity: French opposing English; Protestant versus Catholic; Irish against Scottish. Layered over these seemingly intractable tribal differences were painful memories of violent sectarian strife stretching back through the Rebellions of 1837 and long-standing economic grievances over trade. If this was not enough, a coherent political philosophy for the new country had to be fashioned out of a job lot of competing populist, conservative and classical liberal beliefs. Should the new nation on balance empower local or national legislatures? Was the goal of union individual liberty or social stability? More fundamentally, how, at a time of profound upheaval—a moment when the armed insurrection of previous decades, sectarian strife and linguistic intolerance pressed down on the new synthesis—could Canada's disparate colonies configure themselves anew?

At Confederation, Canada's civic culture was infused with the belief that the vigorous and reasoned expression of ideas could influence the progress of peoples and civilizations. Interlocutors who stood behind prejudice or tradition—to avoid the rough-and-tumble arena of public debate—were perceived as circumventing the civic mechanism through which the best principles and actions revealed themselves. Not only did ideas matter, the process through which they were discussed was of paramount importance. The public good demanded that political actors rise above narrow self-interest and engage each other with intellectual openness and generosity of spirit.

The ethos of civility that permeated Canada at Confederation created a remarkably fluid and versatile political culture. Hard and fast enemies came together in new coalitions. New ideas swept the political field. The civic culture of the day was also energized by the degree to which the architects of Confederation shared an intimate knowledge of history, current events and political philosophy. The common cultural capital that underpinned public discourse functioned as a powerful bulwark against the centrifugal forces of ethnicity, language and religion. Confederation was not just a political triumph of institutions, it was a product of a civic culture of remarkable resilience, creativity and accommodation.

Nevertheless, it was institutions and not the free play of ideas that Canadians came to rely upon in entrenching a common civic culture. From the exploits of the Royal Canadian Mounted Police to the driving of the last spike on the CPR, the country's history is filled with larger-than-life stories of how founding institutions tamed a continent and defined Canada's national character in the process. Unlike our southern neighbour, and in order to be unlike it, we eschewed a national identity founded on a set of ideological principles. Our great political accomplishments—the means through which we articulated our political and civic values—came to be understood in institutional terms. The *Quebec Act*, the hard-won rights of responsible government, and Confederation were not viewed just as political milestones. Rather they encapsulated entire theories of governance, individual rights and the common good. Indeed, our institutions not only represent who we are as a nation, but also indicate a remarkable record of accomplishment and social innovation. When Canada's experience of the last two hundred years is compared with that of the rest of the Western world, we do seem to have good reason to take confidence in our institutions' ability to foster an open and vital civic culture. To be sure, there have been a few isolated and painful incidents. But we have avoided the civil war, revolution and racial oppression that characterized Europe's and our neighbour's experiences of modernity.

This said, recent history suggests that Canadians' civic culture is undergoing a sea change despite the relative health of our institutions. Growing numbers of us now feel alienated from the political process. We are distrustful of government and troubled by the social fragmentation of our communities. At a basic level, the historic bond between the strength of our institutions and the vitality of our civic culture seems to be breaking. As Canada faces the twenty-first century, the civic values that once led us to rely on our institutions to forge a national consensus out of different regional, racial, and linguistic interests seem to be giving way to new, divisive attitudes. When our civic culture seems gripped by lassitude, and the discord of the country seems an all too familiar status quo, how can we configure ourselves anew? How can we restore vitality to our civic culture and help our institutions once again resonate with shared values?

Canada at the onset of the twenty-first century is still the progeny of the remarkable civic culture that achieved Confederation. At a time when our understanding of what it means to be Canadian seems paralyzed by apathy and entrenched grievances, we need to reconnect with the civic philosophy of Canada's founders. We need to inject into our public discourse the enduring principle that there is no truth we cannot tell each other. We need to take confidence in the underlying values of our civic culture and its capacity to contain, even within the most divisive of debates, a spirit of mutual understanding, civility and tolerance. *Great*

Questions of Canada is a reminder of what has long made Canada work: our collective ability to fashion a new vision of the country through generous dialogue about ideas.

Taken together, the thirty-two essays that make up this book provide a new perspective on the challenges of renewing Canada's civic culture and institutions. This collection is based on the premise that the "great questions" that captivated the country's founders and animated the vibrant civic culture of 1860s are still very much with us today: How can we achieve unity? Is there a common Canadian identity? What political institutions should we have? What is our role in world affairs? Discussing these questions will help us step back from the twenty-four-hour news cycle and re-engage these seminal issues.

The resulting perspective on Canada suggests that our current inclination to see our civic culture and institutions as somehow moribund, or devoid of ideas and values, is misplaced. Whether the issue is medicare or the Constitution, our institutions and civic culture are infused with ideas and values that stretch back to the country's founding. Rebuilding our civic culture requires us to reconnect with the historic dialogue we have had about the concepts that animate both our political institutions and our relationships with the world and with one another. Equally important, we need to inject into our national conversation the intellectual passion and public spiritedness that typified Canada at Confederation. In tone and style, the point-counterpoint format of *Great Questions of Canada* demonstrates how the exchange of ideas—conducted in the style of a lively debate—encourages not only good arguments, but better prospects of conciliation.

DOES HISTORY MATTER?

Research abroad and in Canada has questioned the existence of a common public memory. Is this a new trend? Does it matter in an increasingly technologically oriented present? And if something is to be done, what dangers and challenges lie in invigorating a common history?

HISTORY AS VICTIMOLOGY

BY JACK L. GRANATSTEIN

IF THERE WAS EVER ANY argument about this subject, it has surely been brought to an end by events in the former Yugoslavia. The world watched Serbs go to war for Kosovo, an area of little intrinsic value but of supreme interest to their nationality in historical terms. History—the events of a half-millennium ago—mattered.

By the same token, NATO went to war against Belgrade for a combination of historical reasons. Slobodan Milosevic was committing genocide (again) and the world, sensitized by the Holocaust and remembering Serb actions against Croats and Bosnians several years before, could not accept this. Western critics of the war argued, on the other hand, that Kosovo could become another Vietnam—a trap out of which nothing but body bags could come. In other words, history mattered to both sides, though all too often politicians and commentators applied its lessons with a rashness that historians usually hope to avoid.

History matters to Canadians, too. French Canadians cherish the humiliations they suffered at the hands of the *anglais*, and Lucien Bouchard rose to prominence, in substantial part, because he could embody the sense of outraged nationalism such humiliations produce better than anyone else. Peter Lougheed, the long-time Alberta premier, similarly made himself the spokesman for a province that cherished its grievances against Central Canada. The past is important.

But not in our schools. There is scarcely a school system in Canada that obliges its students to learn anything of world history, North American history or European history. The key to understanding our civic institutions, British history, has been eliminated from the classroom because the British are seen as just another ethnic group deserving no special attention.

Worse yet, astonishingly, four provinces have no compulsory Canadian history course in their high schools. Others bury the past in a mishmash of civics, pop sociology, and English as a Second Language, eliminating anything that might offend students, parents, and school trustees, in an attempt to produce an airbrushed past free of warts (except for the officially approved historical sins that can be used for present-day social engineering). In Ontario, until the Tory government in 1999 announced a revised history curriculum, the only compulsory history course was a grade ten offering on "Canada in the Twentieth Century" that epitomized this type of history.

Just as civil servants put process ahead of policy, so have our schools put process over learning. History is hard, and to master the Canadian (or any other) past is difficult. But that is its great virtue, of course. History requires thought, demands wide reading and almost forces those who study it to write. In an age of multiple-choice examinations, few other subjects in our schools any longer demand thinking, reading, and writing. This makes history all the more important.

As bad, the way the past is presently taught is hopelessly confused in its aims. Facts are boring, dates are unimportant, and the past is, by definition, another country for the present-minded, so why bother? What matters, the education theorists say, is that students should learn to read critically and to probe texts for the writers' underlying biases. There is certainly utility in critical reading, but whether one can discern bias without first knowing some hard information is doubtful.

Whether society can function without common cultural capital is also uncertain. For example, how can Canadian voters—and eighteen-year-olds are voters—make rational political choices in this new century without understanding such terms as *British North America Act,* *"Constitution Act," "Charter of Rights and Freedoms," "provincial powers,"* and "Social Union"?

History has a social utility in a nation like ours. Canada is a magnet for millions from all over the world. People choose to immigrate here because this is a land of opportunity, a nation with Western values and ideals, and a past that is attractive. Integrating the children of immigrants from Russia, Bolivia, Hong Kong, Somalia, and Albania into our society ought to be an overriding object of Canadian policy. The values and traditions of Canadian life should be force-fed to them; history should be explained in ways that demonstrate how and why we have regularly settled our disputes without force, how our political system has functioned, and why we have on many occasions gone to war or joined alliances, not for aggressive reasons, but to protect our democratic ideals. Those are the reasons immigrants come here, after all.

But do we teach this past to our newcomers? Not a chance. Our schools are value-free or, at least, value-neutral. Our system is but one of many, and heaven forfend that we should pronounce Western culture superior to any other. Moreover, lest our history upset anyone, we ensure that anything offensive to any group or nation is deleted. Instead, the history that is taught focuses on Canada's many sins: Canadian racism, Canadian sexism, Canadian abuses of human and civil rights—these are all studied at length in a well-intentioned, but misguided attempt to educate children about the need for tolerance.

Tolerance, yes, of course. But what does an approach to the past that concentrates on our (relatively few) sins and all but neglects our (relatively plentiful) virtues do to immigrant children, who must wonder into what kind of monstrous society their parents have plunged them? What does such an approach tell the native-born about their homeland? Somehow in our efforts to be "unbiased" and fair to all, we have distorted our past into one full of sin and error.

Yes, in the past some Canadians have been racist or sexist or have abused governmental powers. Some still are and do. But that is not the whole of the Canadian past, or of our present. Although one could not tell from the way our history is taught, somehow this country became the most favoured nation on earth.

Our teaching of the past, however, focuses on victimology, and Lord knows, we Canadians are all victims: all women have suffered at the hands of men, all aboriginals who attended residential schools were abused, as were all those unfortunates who went to parochial schools, especially those operated by the Christian Brothers. Sometimes these tales are accurate, but only sometimes. Not everyone was or is a victim, despite the clamorous legal claims of the present.

History matters. The way it is taught—or not taught—has shaped a tuned-out generation that can use a computer and surf the Net, but that knows almost nothing about anything of importance, except that anything important must be inexpressibly boring. Kosovo? Immaterial. Social Union? Incomprehensible. The future? Unknowable, but surely bleak.

THE HISTORY THAT MATTERS MOST

BY MICHAEL IGNATIEFF

THE REAL DISPUTE between Jack Granatstein and me isn't whether history matters—it obviously does—or whether it should be taught in Canadian schools—it must. The question is what history? Whose history?

Once upon a time, more than twenty years ago, I set out from Harvard with my newly minted doctorate to teach Canadian history to students at the University of British Columbia in Vancouver. In my innocence, I had supposed that there was a genuinely national history to teach. It was the story of Cartier and Champlain, the Plains of Abraham, Upper and Lower Canada, the struggle for responsible government, and the achievement of Confederation. Try teaching that to students on Canada's West Coast. To them, it was just an interesting fable about a distant land two thousand miles to the east. They didn't begin to believe it was their story until the railway made it to Vancouver. It took a semester for this particular Torontonian to realize that the national history I took for granted was essentially regional—the story of the settlement of what Donald Creighton called "the empire of the St. Lawrence."

The other reason the history I was teaching wasn't a genuinely national history was that it left out almost all of the people. It was a history of the politics, diplomacy, and warfare that led to

23

the creation of British North America and the Canadian political system. While this has to be the core of any national history, it leaves out a lot. Where were the sodbusters, the Prairie settlers? Where were the Ukrainians? Where were their own ancestors, my students wanted to know? Where were the Chinese labourers who built the railway? The people from the subcontinent of India who came out to cut timber? The Japanese who worked in the market gardens of British Columbia's lower mainland?

The history I was teaching them left out what mattered to my students. It didn't help them make sense of the photographs in their family albums or the tales told by their grandmothers and grandfathers. And as for the aboriginal peoples, whose civilization had marked the history of the Pacific Northwest, if my students wanted to study them, they had to head over to the anthropology department. Their achievements—and their tragedy—had no place in the Canadian story.

Things have changed radically since I taught out at UBC. I don't know whether we have a genuinely national history—one that incorporates the five regions of the country—but I do know that the story has become more inclusive. Thanks to the young social historians who came out of graduate school in the sixties and seventies, ordinary people—the immigrants, workers, orphaned children, religious groups, and aboriginal peoples—have come back to the centre of the story, where they belong. Of course, this makes it more difficult to tell Canada's story, for we have to keep asking who the "we" is.

My counterpart, Jack Granatstein, seems to lament this, and to feel that our history genuflects too much to political correctness, to a pious wish to uplift all of our national communities. But this is not political correctness so much as long overdue recognition that Canada's national story has been defined by a constant struggle over who belongs, who is included, who gets the right to use the word "we" and who gets labelled "they."

Professor Granatstein also seems to lament the fragmentation of our common historical understanding, the waning of a sense of a "shared" history. Again, what history? Whose history? Our national experience has been recurrently bedevilled (as well as enriched) by the fact that English and French Canada do not share the same history of 1759. For the English, it is a victory; for the Québécois, a bitter defeat. For more than two hundred years, Canadian politics has been defined by the quarrel over the meaning of the battle on the Plains of Abraham. It is sentimental illusion to suppose that the two communities will ever agree on what it means. At best, we will agree to disagree; we will continue the argument. And the argument—provided it remains civil—will not prevent us from living together and sharing political institutions.

It would be nice if one day Québécois people would admit that the Conquest didn't turn out too badly for them; that the British conquerors actually safeguarded their religion and laws when they imposed a common matrix of British institutions. And it would be nice if the English admitted that the French are not some inconvenient historical anomaly, a troublesome people who have always threatened our unity, but instead that their presence— and the unending argument that goes with it—has defined us both and made us different and actually helps guarantee our joint survival as a distinct people. But we shouldn't count on this kind of shared understanding. History matters to both "founding nations," but we shouldn't suppose it will ever be the same story.

History for Professor Granatstein is primarily about civics, a bracing lesson in patriotism, with little room for tales of suffering or dissent. For me, history is the story of our arguments: French versus English, native-born versus new arrivals, region versus region, rich versus poor, race versus race, religion versus religion. It is also the story of how we managed to resolve these arguments, how we created a way of agreeing to disagree. Jack Granatstein worries that too much emphasis on our disagreements will turn our history into a victimology. Too much emphasis on the negative will turn us into a nation of victims instead of the proud patriots we should be.

I don't think history is—or should be—just a lesson in patriotism. It should be a lesson in truth. And the truth is both painful and many-sided. What kind of history of Canada is it that would exclude the execution of Riel, the *War Measures Act*, the bitterly divisive debates about conscription, the residential schools for aboriginal children? And what kind of history would it be that talked only of these darker and more difficult sides of our past? Just as one-sided as a history that omits them. We all want to love our country; we all want to be reconciled to its past. But reconciliation and love require understanding, and to understand our history, we first need to tell the truth.

Jack Granatstein wants to "force-feed" Canadian history to our immigrants. He seems anxious about whether the centre can hold, as Canada becomes a fully multicultural and multi-ethnic society. I think the centre will hold, provided it knows how to change. These anxieties about immigration are, as Granatstein well knows, old hat in Canada. Doubtless, there were Anglican worthies a century ago who worried about the dreadful things his ancestors and mine were going to do to their cherished idea of Canada.

But here it is Professor Granatstein, not I, who seems to lose faith in our history. In Laurier's day, we took in millions of southern and eastern Europeans. They didn't speak our language; they didn't have the slightest conception of the history of British North America. Four generations later, their descendants are helping to run the country. The same thing will happen to the Caribbeans, the Asians, and the Latin Americans who are now joining the Canadian experiment. Yes, they should learn the history of this country. They should know who Wilfrid Laurier was. They particularly need to understand that we are a nation strengthened, rather than weakened, by competing and contradictory visions of the national experience, and that their vision of who we are and should be matters just as much as the vision of those who were born here.

Having disagreed so sharply, let me, in true Canadian fashion, conclude on a note of agreement. Like Jack Granatstein, I'm not a relativist. I don't believe history is just the stories we happen to tell about it. History is both a set of facts about the past and a set of conflicting interpretations about their meaning. The facts matter, and all Canadians need to know them.

I don't like the idea of a Canada where no one knows who Laurier was, where everyone has forgotten what Pierre Trudeau stood for. We can argue about the facts—and I say the more argument the better—but we are truly done for if we pretend that they do not exist. They do and they set the limits of any arguments we can hope to have. Jack Granatstein is to be warmly congratulated for fighting to make sure that our schools and universities teach us enough good history that we can disagree about what it means.

POSTSCRIPT BY
JACK L. GRANATSTEIN

ONE OF THE JOYS of writing is that no matter how clear a writer tries to be, no matter how explicitly he sets out his position, readers will see in his text whatever they want. To Michael Ignatieff, in his first essay, I appear to want history to be "a civics lesson, a bracing lesson in patriotism, with little room for tales of suffering or dissent." "What kind of history of Canada is it that would exclude...the bitterly divisive debates about conscription?" he asks.

The answer, of course, is bad history. Any history that sets out simply to pound patriotism into children's heads is by definition dreadful, biased, slanted, and twisted. No professional historian I know, and certainly not I, wants to see this happen. The history we teach in the schools should be history, warts and all. And yes, conscription, an issue that tore the nation apart in 1917, 1942, and 1944, should be in the curriculum. As the author who has written more on that subject than anyone else, as the co-author of textbooks that cover that subject at length, I could scarcely say anything else. (After all, I do want my books to sell!)

The history we teach cannot be narrow institutional history; although, like Ignatieff, I believe that this must be "the core of any national history." The history we teach must include the immigrants, the workers, the aboriginal peoples, the religious groups, and the orphans, exactly as Ignatieff says.

But what he does not seem to realize is that the core—what he calls "the politics, diplomacy, and warfare that led to the creation of British North America and the Canadian political system"—has been largely excised from our schools and universities. So, too, has the political, diplomatic, and military history of post-Confederation Canada. The social historians that Ignatieff rightly praises for putting the ordinary people into our history are the same historians who have simultaneously excised the political leaders, diplomats and generals. The bureaucrats who set the curricula in our schools have cheerfully gone along with this for their own social engineering purposes. Where Canadian history is still taught as a compulsory course in high school—in four provinces, it is not!—scant attention is paid to anything but social or regional history. And too much of that social history focuses on the maltreatment of aboriginals and ethnics, the abuse of women, and the evils of capitalism.

In *Who Killed Canadian History?*, published in the spring of 1998, I began with a true story of the first exposure to Canadian history received by the eight-year-old son of friends. In five two-page essays, scratched out in his beginner's handwriting, the boy looked at how Samuel de Champlain, the father of New France, abused his child bride; the extermination of Newfoundland's Beothuks by the white man; the execution of Louis Riel, the "hero of his people," by Ottawa's racist government; the abuse suffered by Canada's first woman doctor at the hands of her male colleagues; and the racist-driven "internment" of Japanese Canadians in 1942 during the Second World War.

I agree that all of these abuses happened and I immediately agree that these issues must be studied. But I oppose the indoctrination of children that our schools presently practise. What did that impressionable boy take away from his first study of Canada's history? That Canada was racist, sexist, and evil. Far from teaching what Michael Ignatieff describes as "a bracing lesson" in civics or patriotism, the schools' focus is always exclusively on the historical ills, on a type of anti-patriotism. "What kind of history would it be that talked only of the darker and more difficult sides of our past?" Ignatieff asks. Bad history, of course, political correctness carried to ludicrous extremes, political correctness that says to Canadians, native-born and recent arrivals, that their nation, past and present, is an abomination. Unfortunately, that is the history that all too often is being taught to Canadian children.

This is the indoctrination of unbalanced historical nonsense filtered through a present-day political agenda. To anyone with eyes to see, Canada is not a failure, but an overwhelming success. Problems, yes; failures, of course; but without question a success.

All I want, all I have ever wanted, for Canadian history is that it be presented to students in a balanced way. I'll readily admit that, when Ignatieff first taught twenty years ago, and when I first taught more than thirty years ago, the teaching of our history was unbalanced. It was the dreary tale of colony to nation and the emphasis was very heavily concentrated on the Central Canadian story. I can understand why his students in British Columbia found this unengaging.

But, unlike the trendy Michael Ignatieff, I believe very strongly that Canadians should know the story of Canada's origins, whether they live in British Columbia or Newfoundland or Quebec. Americans, for example, seem to think it important to teach children about George Washington and the revolt of the thirteen colonies in the long-passed eighteenth century, whether they live in Massachusetts, Arizona, or Oregon. British schools teach Scottish and Welsh children about King John and the Magna Carta, about William the Conqueror and the Battle of Hastings in 1066.

Why shouldn't British Columbia schools teach about the struggles of Québécois to preserve their culture, the *Quebec Act*, the Rebellions of 1837, Louis Joseph Papineau, William Lyon

Mackenzie and William Lyon Mackenzie King? And why shouldn't Ontario schools teach Toronto and Moosonee children about Amor De Cosmos and W.A.C. Bennett, and the Progressives and the Progressive Conservatives? Only in Canada would anyone suggest that a national perspective on the past be left out.

Balance demands that Canadian schools teach about Canada, all of Canada. It demands that the story of the workers and the women be taught, as well as the stories of Mike Pearson, the world wars, conscription, and Canadian-American relations. And, yes, just as Ignatieff says, balance demands that differing interpretations be presented to students for them to argue and fight about. That is how we learn, that is how we come to understand the past, that is how we strive to uncover the truth. History is indeed "the story of our arguments," and history is a lesson in truth—and a lesson about the difficulty of uncovering the truth from a welter of confusing facts and lies and differing interpretations.

No one wants our schools to teach the pablum of an authorized and officially approved version of the past. This is a red herring, a chimera, spread to frighten children and childish adults. There is no such thing as an authorized version of the past in Canada, and there never will be, so long as we remain a democracy where individuals can read what they wish, write what they want, and publish their ideas in a variety of media. There is no single interpretation of the history of French-English relations in Canada, for example, and I know of no competent historian who would suggest that there is or should be. Certainly, I have never argued any such thing. The history I taught my students and the history I write—much of which deals with French-English relations in the contentious periods of wartime—is ordinarily revisionist, arguing a strong thesis and positing (or trying to do so) an argument that challenges conventional wisdom. By delicately suggesting that I want schools to teach one-sided patriotic mush, Michael Ignatieff has set up a straw man and readily demolished it. But this bears no relation to the history I write, the beliefs I hold or the history that I think should be taught in our schools.

Let me be as clear as I can. We need to teach history in our schools. Today we scarcely do, for history (and history teachers!) have been driven out by social studies, civics, geography, English as a Second Language, and a variety of current-events courses that are largely devoted to anti-racism or gender-sensitivity education. These are useful subjects, of course, but we also need to teach about the ancient world and the Middle Ages, about the history of Europe, Africa and Asia, and about the histories of Britain and the United States. The newspapers and television shows talk about globalization as a panacea or threat (depending on where one stands these days), but we are sending Canadians out to do business with scarcely the foggiest notion about why the Serbs, the Indonesians, and the Sri Lankans, or the British, the French, and the Americans act as they do. History has been eliminated in our educational system for more than a generation now, and we are already paying and will continue to pay a heavy price.

This is especially true when we consider our own history. Canadians need to know how we reached our present situation, and they need to understand the forces, factors, and individuals that shaped our present. To state matters in their simplest form, Canadians must learn that history happened. It does us no good to pretend that we have always been peacekeepers, for example, or that somehow Canadians are innately blessed with the ability to teach the world about compromise. We're not. Canadians fought wars in the twentieth century: the South African War, the Great War, the Second World War, the Korean War, the Gulf War, and the Kosovo War. More than 114,000 Canadians died in these conflicts and on peacekeeping operations, and it downgrades their efforts to pretend that we are a uniquely peaceful people. Again, we are not, but we have never fought an aggressive war, which few nations can claim, and we have always fought for our allies and friends and for our beliefs in concepts such as democracy and freedom. Again, few countries can make such a claim.

But we scarcely teach our children anything about war in our schools, and the result is that teachers and students solemnly state that they are pacifist, that Canada will never fight another war, and that, certainly, they would not fight. This is ludicrous and dangerous nonsense, especially as it is uttered not that long since the Gulf War and the war in Kosovo, in both of which Canada participated with overwhelming public support.

Very simply, Canadians need to realize that this nation's history cannot, must not, be twisted out of shape for present-day social engineering purposes. Our schools need to teach the history of Canada and they need to teach more of it, and Canadian history must not be used for indoctrination.

Again, let me be absolutely clear: our history must be presented warts and all. Historians should strive to show where we failed, for example, in the treatment of the aboriginal peoples and the racism that blighted the lives of Chinese and Japanese immigrants to this country. And they should show where we succeeded: the generally peaceful and successful integration of millions of immigrants from all over the world and the nation's enormous efforts to defend freedom in the wars of the terrible twentieth century, to cite only two examples. Historians in our schools (and universities too) should teach social history and political history. They should teach about region and locality and about Canada as a whole. They should be balanced, in other words. Of course, history is innately a contentious subject—that is why it is both fun and dangerous—but it is suicidally stupid to resolve the problems history can pose by not teaching it at all. That, unfortunately, is what Canadian schools have largely done.

Is this argument too difficult to understand? Is what I suggest any different than the kind of history Michael Ignatieff, and any sensible person, would want? The real question that must be addressed is why we Canadians do not teach our own (or any other) national history in our schools. Michael Ignatieff and I could have had a real debate about important matters if he had tried to answer that question instead of flogging a dead horse that no one ever rode.

POSTSCRIPT BY
MICHAEL IGNATIEFF

WHAT IS THE FUNDAMENTAL issue at stake here? What are Jack
Granatstein and I really arguing about? The argument is not really
about history, whether it matters, whether it should be taught in
Canadian schools, and whether it should contain a strong dose of
constitutional and political content. We agree about all this. Jack
deserves the thanks of all historians, indeed of all Canadians for
drawing attention to the scandalous neglect of the discipline in
our public schools.

The question between us, therefore, is not whether history
matters and should be taught, but why. We seem to have differing
views about what history can contribute to the country: to its
unity, coherence, and quality of citizenship. He never says so
explicitly, but Jack Granatstein seems to feel that Canada's "common cultural capital" is frittering away, that we are failing to teach
the core values and ideas that will keep the country together in the
future. I'm less sure that Canada is in any kind of jeopardy. I doubt
it was ever united in the way he supposes; indeed, I'm not sure any
country is as united as he supposes. To the degree that countries
do have "common cultural capital," it is made up of the history of
their disagreements.

To clarify this debate, I can see three distinct questions: Do
Canadians possess "common cultural capital"? Should we be trying to strengthen it? Is the country jeopardized if we don't?

What do we mean by "common cultural capital"? It's Jack
Granatstein's phrase, and I presume he means a set of

understandings, widely shared by Canadians, about how the country came to be, what its basic rules are and what it stands for. From these understandings flow certain ways of behaving towards each other: because we understand each other, we are more tolerant, more civil, more knowledgeable about our country and the choices it faces. Common cultural capital helps the country hold together, because it makes us better citizens. So there seems to be a lot at stake here.

Let me concede what I can to this view. It's hard to imagine Canada functioning without some shared understandings—the rules of democracy, the rule of law, a shared knowledge of the geography and how the political system works, or is supposed to work—and certain habits of mind that go with these understandings—a willingness to argue out our differences instead of reaching for a gun and a belief that everybody should try to stand on their own two feet, coupled with a view that those who genuinely can't are entitled to some help.

There isn't anything very Canadian about these understandings: most Western liberal democracies would have much the same common ground. What is distinctive about our story is that we are British North America. We are subjects of the British Crown and not citizens of a republic. We admire but do not form part of the great Jeffersonian-Madisonian constitutional experiment to the south. We do not believe in a constitutional right to bear arms and we view with disbelief the American convention that allows every householder to possess firearms. We think that public taxation should provide for health care and that it is wrong for decent medical care to depend on the size of our bank balances.

In constitutional terms, our rights culture provides quite distinctive protections for linguistic and aboriginal minorities. Unlike either the French republican tradition or the American one to the south, we try to balance collective rights for these groups with equal rights for individuals. We have a hard time doing so, but there is little doubt that the political result is a quite distinctive constitutional system that makes Canada one of the most devolved and decentralized federations in the world.

This is a particular view of what makes Canada different, one that puts the emphasis on politics and rights, rather than on the usual areas: our frozen wastes, our noble forests, our peerless resources. It is history, not nature, in other words, that makes Canada distinctive.

Jack Granatstein must be right to suppose that a consciousness of these facts—a historical sense of what it means to be a Canadian—would contribute to an active and committed sense of citizenship, a willingness to speak up and fight when Canada risks being sold down the river. Who would deny that we need something more than a shared willingness to play by the rules to hold Canada together? We need a sense that our country has a particular history in order to know why it matters that we preserve her institutions.

But let us not overdo this. All of us have met devoted and patriotic Canadians who had only the slimmest idea of our common history. I daresay many of those extraordinary young men who gave their lives in France in the First World War died for a country whose basic historical chronology was only dimly in their minds. Historical knowledge of our country is a wonderful thing, but it is not a precondition for civic virtue or civic sacrifice.

If we believe it is, we can all too easily conclude that the country is going to hell in a handcart. We can surrender to the kind of nostalgic pessimism that is apt to seize anyone over fifty who surveys the apparently appalling ignorance of the younger generation. Historical ignorance is unattractive, and we should fight it as Jack Granatstein has done, but it is a *folie de grandeur* to believe the country is done for if our citizenry can't repeat the names of all our prime ministers back to Confederation, the major battles since 1759, and the key provisions of the BNA Act.

Most of the time, our country holds together perfectly well on the basis of a very shallow set of historical understandings. What actually holds us together is something altogether more prosaic: people doing their jobs. Canada, like any other country, has an incredibly complex division of labour and all of our actions—such as going to the store for a newspaper and a pint of milk—depend for their success on other anonymous Canadians—the newspaper-delivery man, the farmer, the dairy people—doing their jobs. We work for each other, as Adam Smith said two centuries ago, without much common sentiment or attachment. Indeed, we reproduce the social solidarity upon which order and prosperity depend without aiming for much more than our own advancement, and certainly without any very large amount of civic pride. Common cultural capital—like being honest, being on time, doing the best we can in the circumstances—is essential to the daily reproduction of our division of labour. But shared historical understanding comes low down in the ranks of preconditions for this type of order.

This type of order, it will be said, has nothing to do with politics and national unity. Yet without this boring, low-level reproduction of daily life, we wouldn't have a country. And this division of labour cuts right across the political divisions we do have. Indeed, it is why so many of our political arguments seem irrelevant to most people: language issues or aboriginal rights or federal-provincial imbroglios seem to have nothing to do with the patient, molecular reproduction of ordinary life. For these ordinary tasks, next to zero historical understanding is required, yet the country would collapse if they were not accomplished.

This is a disagreeable thought to any historian, since it implies that computer-programming or driving skills, or knowing how to milk cows (to get that pint of milk to the grocery store), matter just as much as historical knowledge. But it is a thought that must be entertained, before we proclaim how essential our discipline and way of seeing are to a country that shares our view that history matters—but not as much as we think it does.

So we do have common cultural capital, but we share it with other countries, and it is not as distinctive, not as Canadian, and not as historical as we like to think. It is a product of our history, but it might still work to keep us civil even if we had mostly forgotten where it came from. Or, to put it in a more provocative way, we might be more civil if we could forget our history a little more completely. There are countries with too much history and too much remembering. The former Yugoslavia, for example, is a country made toxic by too much history. The young militiamen methodically engaged in ethnic cleansing in Bosnia, whether Serb, Croat or Muslim, never lacked for a deeply felt historical justification for what they were doing, crafted from some murderous historical fiction lovingly handed from father to son. An extreme example admittedly, but one worth bearing in mind when we Canadians lament the shallowness of our historical memory. It is shallow because it does not haunt us. It is slight because it does not keep us awake at night. For that we should be exceedingly grateful.

To the degree that we do remember our historical past, it hurts as much as it helps us. That inscription on Quebec licence plates—*Je me souviens* (I remember)—implies that Québécois identity should be a matter of keeping faith with the old quarrels, the old injustice, the old memories of hurts and slights. Jack Granatstein would be displeased by the suggestion, but if that is what "I remember" actually means, I'd prefer my licence plate to read "I've forgotten."

He doesn't say this, but why else would he want to be "force-feeding" (his word) a core curriculum of Canadian political and institutional history to immigrants and adolescent Canadians? You only "force-feed" ideas that you think are going to make an essential difference.

I share his concern about the fact that history is not taught in Canadian schools the way it was or the way it should be. Like him, I don't want history reduced to victimology. I don't want it to bow to every current fashion of political correctness. I don't want to see it elbowed out of the schools because other things—computers, business studies, whatever—seem more relevant. All this is common ground between us.

What I refuse to believe is that widely diffused knowledge of Canadian history is essential to Canadian unity and some kind of necessary prerequisite for adequate citizenship. There are many forms of good citizenship, and not all require specific historical knowledge. Neighbourliness, civic courage, willingness to serve in political office, community pride: all of these can be enhanced by historical consciousness, but they do not require it.

We do not just inherit history; we make it together. It is not some constantly diminishing stock that must be replenished or we will suddenly be strangers to each other. Our common cultural capital is not depleting; it is simply changing very rapidly, as our demographic composition, economic structure, and technology change. Canada recurrently wakes up and doesn't recognize itself. There is nothing new about this. Because we are a lucky country, one that the whole world wants to come to, we are a country that changes all the time, and because we change all the time, we recurrently worry that we are losing ourselves. These worries are

40

real, but teaching a lot more Canadian history in our schools is not going to make them go away. I don't see Canadian history as a branch of civics. We don't need that and it would kill the discipline Jack Granatstein and I both love.

ARE WE A NATION OF TOO MANY IDENTITIES?

In the last century women have been enfranchised, attitudes towards First Nations peoples have changed and the entire ethnic composition of Canada has shifted markedly. How have personal and official conceptions of identity changed over time? What political and cultural changes will Canada's identity revolution bring next?

DREAMING OF OTHER LANDS

BY NEIL BISSOONDATH

EACH WORD PREGNANT with emotion, he spoke of Ireland as of a long-lost and irretrievable love. The music in particular, he said. "Danny Boy" knotted his throat and sent shivers down his spine. It was his love theme to the past.

To the distant past, actually. He himself had never been to Ireland, nor had his parents. His grandparents had been from there—and if the sounds of Ireland moved him to tears it was, he felt, because the place was rooted within him with an almost genetic intensity. Canada was his home, but nothing about it could move him to this degree.

The man's feeling was undoubtedly genuine. Yet, to me, his logic was flawed. "Danny Boy" sends shivers up and down my spine, too, and the closest thing I have to Irish heritage is an aunt by marriage—and even she is now divorced from my uncle.

We in Canada have done an abysmal job of appreciating our own history. We know that our first prime minister was fond of drink; that the man who guided us through the Second World War had peculiar relationships with his dog and his dead mother. The railroad, once a symbol of national achievement, has lost its romance. We know that history has not been kind to our native peoples—we feel either guilt over the evils visited on them or resentment over the demands made by their descendants. If we are at all aware of history, it is to wish that it had been different, better, more humane. Our historical memory, then, is at best meagre, almost a psychological oubliette that robs us of heroes and leaves us only flawed forefathers. We find hardly any reason for pride in our accomplishments. In our own eyes, we barely exist.

Our ignorance of ourselves has led us to make a fetish of the foreign heritages and identities that now populate our social landscape. Although this landscape is more varied, interesting, and divided than ever before, the only pasts that count are those of elsewhere—mythologized, exoticized, distant enough to accommodate romantic notions of dream and loss. "Danny Boy," "Island in the Sun," "Dark Eyes," and any number of songs will move you, not because they appeal to human emotion, but because they touch the only part of you that you believe to be real. Your Canadianness is only skin deep.

Identity is shaped in essentially two spheres: the private and the public. The private identity is a crystal mosaic of constantly shifting pieces. It can be grasped for only a moment before it slips away, reshaping itself into something subtly altered: by circumstance, by experience, by information gained, and belief proven or disproven. To know oneself is a constantly evolving process: there is no one answer. This is the essential, living identity, shaped by tales of the family odyssey that help individuals locate themselves in time and place, the personal mythology that tells you who you are.

The public identity is a more wilful construct shaped through collective social attitudes and structures, and, on a shallower level, through flags, anthems, speeches meant to stir rather than inform. We feel it when the anthem is played for a winning athlete; when, abroad, we meet a stranger whose strangeness evaporates when we discover a shared nationality and frame of reference. Public identity is, in the end, largely a matter of shared reference—the common ground of the "we." Increasingly in Canada we have dragged private identity into the public domain by using government policy to engineer it into various shapes. Curious, really, when you consider that a nation that has long believed the state to have no place in the bedrooms of the nation would tolerate such interference in the identities of the nation. All "national costumes" are officially recognized in an effort to create a mosaic. But parading around in such costumes—and I mean this figuratively as well—is theatre; it is a child's fantasy of glamour. Flower arrangements in the living room may be appealing, but they have nothing to do with the solidity of the foundations below.

Between the private and public identities there is constant interaction, sometimes soothing, sometimes scathing. While the private can be damaged by the public—history is full of decent people who subordinate the self to the demands of public duty; the tank sometimes crushes the man who stands defiantly before it—the public remains even more vulnerable. In the sixties and early seventies, American public identity was battered by the radical assertion of the private. By the eighties, the hollow concept of the New Soviet Man had been demolished by rugged private identities unwilling to live the lie. The primacy of the private identity became evident.

Canada's public identity continues to be built on opposition ("We aren't like them"), on institutions (medical and employment insurance, welfare, old-age pensions), and on theatrical display (mainly ethnic celebrations). But they don't care how much or how little we resemble them; our public institutions are crumbling, and the costumes, dancing and singing have no meaning beyond entertainment and folklore. This is fragile ground on which to build a cohesive country.

Meeting basic needs goes only so far in fostering a sense of belonging. Distributing free flags is a politician's answer; painting a Canada Day maple leaf on your face is a clown's. If our neighbours to the south (and some of our co-citizens in Quebec) engage in such antics, it isn't to manufacture pride; the pride is already there, the flag-waving merely a way of displaying it.

Instead, we have to allow ourselves to be dazzled by our country, by the wonders that can never be diminished by the political and linguistic squabbling that plagues us like a cancer. We have to learn to see beyond our comfortable limits, be they religious, racial, ethnic, or linguistic. Public policy has a role in showing us not just the evils of the past and the quandaries of the present, but their glories, too. A country without a past or with one demeaned, such as we have allowed ourselves to become, is condemned to a fractious present and an uncertain future, with a citizenry dreaming—ironically—always of elsewhere.

Despite our foreign aid programs and our record in peace-keeping, Canada is a country greatly diminished since the Second World War. The truth is, we carry little weight in the world. Were the Canadian state to disappear tomorrow, many beyond our borders would notice but few would mourn. We have, to some extent, become, as a character in V.S. Naipaul's novel *A Bend in the River* says harshly of us, a hoax: "They thought they were part of the West, but really they had become like the rest of us who had run to them for safety. They were like people far away, living on other people's land and off other people's brains, and that was all they thought they should do."

It was not always so. We have drifted into this state. To pull ourselves out of it we must begin by returning the private and public identities to their proper domains, so that each may grow and strengthen. The two mythologies will eventually find common ground. Then the rest will follow: the collective sense that we, secure in our individual selves, all share in and belong to a large, old, and ongoing enterprise. From out of our gentle chaos will emerge a country unimagined, with purpose beyond survival and influence beyond rhetoric. Only then will we—and the world—be convinced that we truly exist.

BOATS, NOT BIRTHRIGHTS (1999)

BY NAOMI KLEIN

NO.

Nine years ago, an unknown Manitoba MLA named Elijah Harper held up an eagle feather and spoke that single word. With it, he did more than bring down the Meech Lake Accord. He also gave us the perfect personification of the role in which natives, immigrants and even, at times, women are cast in Canadian political theatre: as refuseniks.

For many minorities, Canadian political life is less an experience of day-to-day inclusion than of long stretches of neglect punctuated by dramatic moments of refusal. Diversity in Canada is the right to dig in your heels and say no. Think of how the Mohawks resisted that golf course in Oka or how the National Action Committee on the Status of Women campaigned against the Charlottetown Accord. Think also of the Innu and Cree opposition to Quebec hydroelectric projects, the Lubicon Cree's boycott campaign against Daishowa's logging and the showdown at Gustafsen Lake.

All of these rare instances when minority issues took centre stage manifested themselves as jarring interruptions, often inspiring suppression. All were blockades, in one form or another. All seemed to come as a surprise—as if another, parallel Canada had materialized out of thin air.

It is sometimes argued that we Canadians suffer because we don't know our history. But perhaps we know our history all too well—or rather one big, blinding chapter of it. That chapter, of course, is the one tracing back the essential struggle between the English and the French.

It may seem strange to bring up the unity question in a discussion of identity politics, but they are two sides of the same coin. Identity politics have been all but crushed under the colossal weight of the two largest and most vocal identities on the national landscape: the English and the French.

Many on the right are fond of claiming that ours is a "victim culture." It's true that Canadians are expert whiners, but it's misleading to transplant to our country the political correctness rhetoric of the United States. In the U.S., those vying for political and cultural representation are indeed ethnic minorities, women, and gays and lesbians. In Canada, however, we have an indigenous victim hierarchy. Ours is based entirely on grievances with the logistics of the nation itself: Torontocentrism, Quebec sovereignty, Western and Eastern alienation—problems that can't be solved unless someone moves the Rockies or sinks Montreal.

So the question is not whether Canada's identity has changed since the first Dominion census documented the existence of 125 Jews and eleven "Hindoos." Of course it has. As recently as 1947, 80 per cent of Toronto's inhabitants were of British descent. Today, 42 per cent of Toronto's population is non-white. The real question is why this radical transformation of the population has failed to translate into an equally radical transformation of Canada's sense of self. Why, given the level of public subsidy it receives to portray contemporary Canadian culture, does the CBC do a worse job of reflecting ethnic diversity than the FOX network? More fundamentally, why can't debates about immigration policy, native land claims and pay equity seem to compete with the national preoccupation with unity?

The reason is simple. Canadians may be enthusiastic about political correctness, but once the newspapers have dealt with their Toronto bias, once the television producers have balanced their panels with someone from each coast, once the conference organizers have fussed over simultaneous French–English translation, there is little "correctness" left over for anyone else.

Plainly put, the most vocal oppression junkies in Canada dwell at the very centre of the power elite. Two of our national political parties—including the Official Opposition—are the offspring of this culture of geographic and linguistic complaint. If Lucien Bouchard, the Alberta oil barons, and everyone living in Atlantic Canada are the dispossessed (and have the political and media clout to blare their grievances across the country), how can unemployed African-Canadians in Nova Scotia, underpaid Chinese garment workers in Toronto, or suicidal teens on native reserves ever hope to capture our attention? At least in the United States, the disenfranchised have the cold comfort of facing off against their oppressors. Canada's disenfranchised minorities must first convince their oppressors to stop crying victim themselves.

This warped identity turf war may explain why, while the female vote has become an American political obsession, it remains on the back burner in Canada. Despite feminist breakthroughs in the professions, women can't seem to shatter the glass ceiling over Parliament Hill: although women make up 42 per cent of administrators and managers in Canadian workplaces, they are only 19 per cent of our politicians, well behind the United States' 30 per cent.

The fierce competition for victim status may also explain the shameful indifference to military and police violence against minorities. I'm thinking, for instance, of the tanks rolling into Gustafsen Lake, the police killing of native protester Dudley George at Ipperwash Provincial Park, the RCMP's fatal shooting of Connie Jacobs and her son Ty at the Tsuu T'ina Reserve in Alberta and the police shootings of black youth in Toronto, Montreal, and Vancouver. The outrage sparked by these events pales in comparison with the mass indignation provoked by the use of pepper spray on mostly white university students outside the Vancouver APEC summit.

It should come as no surprise that this jockeying for victim position is at its most bullish in Quebec, ground zero of the unity debate. Though I consider Quebec nationalism to be legitimate, one side effect of this slow-motion revolt has been a propensity among Quebec nationalists to regard multiculturalism with deep and ungenerous suspicion. From the start, the policy was viewed, to use René Lévesque's words, as a dark plot "to obscure 'the Quebec business.'"

The sentiment is alive and well. When Jacques Parizeau blamed "money and the ethnic vote" for his referendum loss, he was stating unequivocally that French Quebecers are Canada's only legitimately aggrieved minority, the "white niggers" of North America that Pierre Vallières famously wrote about. And when Parizeau added, "We know who we are," you can bet that Quebec's ethnic minorities and Jews knew perfectly well who, in his eyes, they were not: real Quebecers.

So there has been no "identity revolution" in Canada—if anything, there has been a devolution, with the old battles of Confederation occupying even more space in the national discourse. Until we stop fighting that war between France and Britain circa 1759, we will never see an "identity revolution" befitting the country's demographic evolution. Put more bluntly, until the core questions of nationality have been resolved, everything else will be secondary.

Is it possible to break this stalemate? Of course. In the optimistic afterglow of Expo 67, Canada enjoyed a level of national self-confidence it has yet to recapture. The spectre of Quebec separation did not go away (indeed, separatism reached a militant status in this period), but even that was unable to take away our broader confidence that Canada had a legitimate and indisputable place in the world. It seems not coincidental, then, that the early seventies brought several breakthroughs in the enfranchisement of women and minorities: Pierre Trudeau's famous 1967 statement that the state had "no place in the bedrooms of the nation," the 1970 Royal Commission on the Status of Women, and the 1971 *Multiculturalism Act*. Those were heady days when Canada was building something, instead of just protecting, defending or dismantling.

When Canada stepped back from its narcissistic quest for a national identity, it could, finally, see the identities of its citizens. It is a lesson worth remembering.

POSTSCRIPT BY
NEIL BISSOONDATH

"THE ESSENTIAL TASK IN TEACHING 'toleration'," Michael Ignatieff writes in his brilliant study of ethnic conflict, *The Warrior's Honour*, "is to help people see themselves as individuals, and then to see others as such; that is, to make problematic that untaught, unexamined fusion of personal and group identity on which nationalist intolerance depends."

Not long ago, I was invited to France as a member of the Quebec delegation to the Paris Book Fair, where the province was guest of honour. We were sixty in all, mainly francophones but some anglophones, too, with "ethnics" both visible and invisible. During one of the many receptions, a woman said to me in the nicest possible way, "Monsieur, you do not look like a Québécois." Her remark was amusing, for it made clear that she had learned an unexpected lesson.

A glance at the massive media coverage given to the Quebec presence at the fair would have revealed—along with such lights as Yves Beauchemin, Marie Laberge, Gaétan Soucy, Jacques Godbout, and Lise Bissonnette—the likes of Dany Laferrière (of Haitian origin), Ying Chen (of Chinese origin), Sergio Kokis (of Brazilian origin), David Homel (of Jewish-American origin), Trevor Ferguson (an anglophone Quebecer) and me. All of these—to, one suspects, the chagrin of certain nationalist politicians—are what today's Québécois look and sound like: individuals of varying backgrounds, colour, religion, and language—but individuals first and foremost who have chosen their place of residence and refined their loyalties on the basis of their own perspectives.

Not long after my return from Paris, the Bloc Québécois, in search of a raison d'être, announced a debate on who is a Quebecer. Premier Lucien Bouchard, barely hiding his irritation, wrote the whole matter off by declaring, as had René Lévesque before him, that anyone who lives in Quebec is a Quebecer. (This is at best a flawed if well-meaning fiction, for it implies that the Quebecer who moves out of the province is no longer a Quebecer; surely anathema to anyone, such as the premier, who sees the existence of a Québécois people as justification for independence.) But Premier Bouchard was signalling his insistence—and, with reservations, I believe him to be sincere—on not playing the perilous politics of division.

This idea of inclusion was, however, the one explicitly rejected on referendum night in 1995 by Jacques Parizeau when he blamed the narrow defeat on money and the ethnic vote. His outburst, evoked by Naomi Klein in her first essay, was an expression of classic ethnic nationalism. But it was also a vision of a society multiculturally divided, the mosaic turned suddenly vicious. Parizeau's virulence revealed the expediency of paeans to ethnic diversity. Ethnicity is praiseworthy only so long as it is profitable—l'ethnicité rentable, in other words. The mosaic, then, is clearly a tool for manipulation—by every manner of politician.

Parizeau was immediately forced to resign as premier and leader of the Parti Québécois. Even though maimed, he still has admirers, and continues buzzing around like an annoying wasp, flying from his nest within the moribund Bloc Québécois to make occasional sorties against Premier Bouchard. His intemperate remarks, however, have made clear the fault lines that threaten the cohesion of the PQ.

It would be a mistake to cast Parizeau as paradigm for Quebec or its nationalism. The fault lines have not closed and may yet lead to irreparable fracture. The reason is simple: the old ethnic vision of Quebec is on the run, chased by a civic nationalism that searches out the similarities between people rather than stressing the differences between them. Ironically, this new nationalism— less ideological, more social in character, shared by many federalists—is the result of the very success of nationalist endeavours such as Bill 101, the language law.

The new Quebec, born of the Quiet Revolution and its astonishing changes, has created a generation of people confident in themselves and their place in the world. Apart from political activists, few of them are driven by ideology or resentment. They feel no obligation to praise the songs of Gilles Vigneault or the plays of Michel Tremblay. They are as likely to read the *New York Times* as *Le Devoir*. And the music they enjoy is more likely to be in English than French, with a healthy dose of world music thrown in. While France is important to them, they do not seek validation from Paris. Many of them speak enthusiastically of Toronto (!). They are a generation of people who know who they are—francophone North Americans. They take their identity for granted, and get on with their lives.

This new Quebec has put legislation and structures in place to ensure just treatment of its diverse population. Premier Bouchard, spiritually of the new generation, recently announced that 25 per cent of a thousand new civil-service posts will be reserved for anglophones and other minorities. No matter how one may feel about such discriminatory hiring practices (I believe in old-fashioned merit evaluated on a level playing field where race, colour, and ethnicity play no part), it is a sign of Quebec's inclusive civic nationalism flexing its muscles.

Few, I suspect, take the Bloc debate seriously. There is nothing to be gained from it. Undeniable, though, is that Parizeau's ethnic vision of Quebec coincides neatly with the multicultural vision prevalent in the rest of the country: a public sphere ethnically divided, easy prey to praise or vilify, as events dictate. In his bluster, Parizeau divided society into non-ethnic and ethnic, those who fully belong and those who do not—precisely as multiculturalism has always done. He shares, then, the view of the mosaic—and a mosaic, remember, is composed of different tiles separated by a band of adhesive: precisely what Toronto immigration expert Tim Rees described in a recent issue of *Time* magazine when he said, "We're living side by side, but not together."

Recently, while I was in England, I had a surprising conversation with a man in his mid-sixties. He had left his homeland of Jamaica when he was seventeen, establishing himself in London. He owned a "little business" importing fruit and vegetables from Jamaica, and had seen his son and daughter through Cambridge University. With an accent so light it was almost untraceable, he spoke of the travelling he had done through Europe and, in 1996, to North America. He had been impressed with Montreal, where he had seen the kind of cultural blending and crossbreeding he loved in London, but had not thought much of Toronto, where he had sensed a kind of isolationism, with the various ethnic groups too jealous of their specificities to offer themselves to others, to open up, to influence, and be influenced. The isolation bothered him; it seemed an approach to life that was small and static and backward-looking. The city struck him as parochial.

His view, even if gained from a brief and somewhat superficial visit, surprised me. Well-spoken and thoughtful, he was not an obviously sophisticated man—his children's education far exceeds his own. Yet he had travelled, he had enjoyed the world: the islands of the Caribbean, yes, for which he retained a particular fondness, but many other places, too. Nowhere did he feel himself a stranger, an alien, an outcast. In Toronto, he had not swallowed the simplistic propaganda of the city authorities or the starry-eyed superficiality of the citizenry. Living in London, he had something enviable with which to compare, and on the level of human inter-action, from the viewpoint of cultural and artistic alchemy, Montreal was, in his view, evolving into something new and unpredictable while Toronto had, to a great extent, failed to profit from its even greater human possibilities.

He had brought up his children, he said, to think of them-selves as neither Jamaican nor British, but rather as people of the world. They were individuals, he stressed, and had to be viewed and treated as such, wherever in the world they found themselves. To fail to recognize their individual abilities—his son, with a tal-ent for chemistry and a taste for the quiet life; his daughter, with her sights on a career in international law and a touch too vibrant social life—was a betrayal, he felt, of their human potential. To treat them as Jamaicans or Brits and not as a young man or young woman of particular talents was to limit them and diminish their role and place in the world. And how sad that would be. He, after all, had gone in search of the world, had found it to his liking and would not accept that the world, or parts of it, would diminish his children with a narrow view of who they were.

Organized society—the collective—is necessary to the devel-opment of human potential. It is society that attends to the well-being of those who choose to belong to it, providing a framework within which individuals and families can develop their abilities, construct their lives, claim their place in the larger human adventure, all with the assurance of a certain measure of safety.

Yet the collective, by its very nature, also has the ability to smother specificities, the individual needs and initiatives that push at its boundaries. Rebels, after all, are always the product of conformity, people who feel themselves confined by a parochialism invisible to those enmeshed in it. It is a danger not unique to Canada; indeed, we hardly see it as a danger. And yet, one has to travel only a little to see how we admire ourselves more than the world does. When we rush to involve our military in peacekeeping duties throughout the world, we indulge in a measure of self-delusion when we think that the world applauds. We are for the most part applauding ourselves. Our collective, which is really a collective of ethnic collectives, has blinded us to its inevitable parochialism, from which we can escape only when we understand that the individual has far greater value, in terms of a universal civilization, than any group. Too often, the "we are" (and its alienating cousin "they are") overwhelms the "I am," smothering human distinctiveness in the name of a greater visionary good. This is what Parizeau was doing on referendum night. This is what that man in London fears would be the fate of his children and their sense of self—their identity—in a society devoted to collective vision.

As a human being and a novelist, I believe that while identity emerges from various sources, it nevertheless belongs exclusively to the individual. Out of the self realized as fully as possible—by realizing, for instance, that the acquisition of marketplace skills is merely one rudiment of a real education—will come a citizenry accepting, and not merely tolerant, of each other. Only then will people begin to live together, sharing a common purpose, seeing each other not as exotics contained within separate mosaic tiles, but rather as fellow Canadians to whom they owe, and from whom they must expect, the full respect that is their due as human beings.

Moreover, in a world made perilous by unrelenting, multi-faceted arrogance, the ideals and institutions bequeathed to us by Western liberal traditions—the essential freedoms they affirm—remain the best guarantors of the alchemy indispensable to the development of individual identity. No other tradition so favours individuals in all their complexity.

"The function of liberal society," Michael Ignatieff writes, "is not merely to teach the noble fiction of human universality, but to create individuals, sufficiently robust in their own identity, to live by that fiction." Individuals, then, must transcend their ethnicity, as a society must de-emphasize it. The mosaic dream is flawed, leading the society that briefly escaped a stultifying parochialism in the sixties into a new kind of parochialism. Canada, a country that uneasily defines itself through the collective of its ethnic communities, must come to grips with the imperative of the noble fiction.

POSTSCRIPT BY
NAOMI KLEIN

NEIL BISSOONDATH WROTE that we in Canada have made such a fetish of other cultures and traditions that, for many of us, "Canadianness is only skin deep." Our "real" selves are rooted in idealized versions of elsewhere, anywhere but here.

The description struck a chord with me. As the child of two Jewish Americans of Eastern European descent, I have often looked elsewhere (to the United States, Israel, Europe) and felt the strange arbitrariness of nationality, felt it to be very unreal indeed. Many of my friends share this feeling of disconnect: one is the child of a Japanese mother and a British father who dreams of New York; another the daughter of Indian immigrants who can't believe any child of theirs would leave the comforts of Canada to do aid work in South Africa; yet another is the son of Italian parents who have, after twenty-seven years in Canada, packed their bags and returned to the small town in Calabria where they were born. Caught between the lands of our ancestors, the countries of our birth and the cities of our work, our uncertain identities mirror the uncertainty at the centre of Canadian life. Ours is a country unsure of what it stands for, filled with people unsure of whether they are truly home.

Mr. Bissoondath suggests that the superficiality of our Canadianness flows from ignorance: we lack identity as a nation because we have no connection to our past. But what if, in trying to forge a deeper connection with this place, the past is not our friend, but our enemy? What if to know Canada's history—not the feel-good, heroic version, but the messy, often wrenching truth—is to know that one's inclusion in this country has only ever been skin deep?

For many Canadians, particularly those who are not of British or French descent, that is exactly what they would find if they looked at our nation's past, and even at much of its present. Canada has forged an identity grounded in a lie. The lie is the one that tells us that we possess an essential national character beyond our common history of stolen land and immigration. This is the lie of the "Two Founding Nations" paradigm, the one at the centre of Canada's national discourse, the one at the heart of the unity debate and the persistent squabbles about who and what is really Canadian.

The late Robert F. Harney, a historian and professor of ethnic studies at the University of Toronto, wrote that in our narratives of how official multiculturalism came to be, there is "a sense of the intrusion of the ethnic groups into an antique struggle between the real Canadians/Canadiens." Historically, immigrants are the interrupters, the ones, though needed for the heavy labour involved in industrializing a vast land such as ours, seen mostly as a threat to some essential, undefinable Canadianness. For the first half of the twentieth century, Canadian opinion and policies on immigration were openly torn between the need to increase our population and the equally pressing need to appear to be protecting an ethnically pure Canada. Nowhere have these two forces been more at odds than in Quebec, where the culture is under a perpetual state of both real and imagined siege. The French language czar Camille Laurin ruthlessly summed up the message so many newcomers still receive when he said that immigrants to Canada are entering a "fully formed nation"—they are free to look, but not touch.

This idea, usually more delicately expressed, has been present throughout our history and has fuelled some of our most shameful national policies—all created, in their own way, to save the "real" Canada from colours and customs not of its own design. The drive towards ethnic purity was behind the *Chinese Exclusion Act* of 1923 that radically restricted Chinese immigration to Canada until 1947. For three decades, this same drive caused native children to be seized from their homes and placed in the care of white families, a practice that reached its peak in the so-called Sixties Scoop. Similarly, the perceived need to protect a static, unchanging Canada from the alien hordes resulted in rigged medical examinations that kept many African-Americans out of Canada before the First World War. It was also the cowardly thinking behind the "none-is-too-many" policy towards Jewish refugees during the Holocaust, and behind the internment of 21,000 Japanese Canadians during the Second World War.

More recent examples abound, signalling to minority Canadians that they are here only on a guest pass. It's not just Jacques Parizeau, and his revealing "we know who we are" remark on referendum night. A similar xenophobia reared its head in the tantrums thrown over the wearing of turbans in the Legion and the RCMP. It's there, too, in the way we whine about the "brain drain" to the United States, while exiling countless Ph.D.s from India and Africa to the front seat of our urban taxicabs, refusing to recognize their credentials.

This painful history of small and large exclusions is the reason Canada lacks the common ground of "we," to use Mr. Bissoondath's term. Too often, the "we" splinters into "us" and "them" at the first sign of trouble, as the four boatloads of Chinese immigrants quickly learned upon their arrival in British Columbia during the summer of 1999. The language chosen to describe the boat people was not the language of a country built by travellers on boats like these, but rather the language of invasion: they were outlaws, queue jumpers, migrants. Conspicuously absent from the discussion was any recognition that Canada is, in fact, a nation of proud mutts, outcasts, and adventurers—or that welcoming poor and needy immigrants is part of what it means to be Canadian.

Perhaps it's a problem less of policy than mythology. In the absence of powerful narratives and symbols of immigration (our "official multiculturalism" is no match for the resonance of the Statue of Liberty or Ellis Island), these huddled masses were treated as criminals, incarcerated for months while the nation hid behind the rhetoric of law and order.

According to novelist Bharati Mukherjee, it is this mythology gap that accounts for the most substantial difference between American and Canadian attitudes towards immigration (not the more common "melting pot" versus "mosaic" theory). In the U.S., rags to riches narratives about immigration and self-transformation occupy the very centre of the American Dream, whereas they are only of marginal importance in Canada. Put another way, Americans welcome their immigrants with the sloppy bear hug implicit in the Statue of Liberty (an embrace, admittedly, that frequently conceals a knife in the back). In Canada, more often than not, we greet immigration by looking at our shoes, or by politely looking the other way.

Comparing the years she spent living in Canada to her current status as an American citizen, Mukherjee writes, "In Canada, I was frequently taken for a prostitute or shoplifter, frequently assumed to be a domestic, praised by astonished auditors that I didn't have a 'sing-song' accent. The society itself, or important elements in that society, routinely made crippling assumptions about me, and about my 'kind.' In the United States, however, I see myself in those same outcasts." Moving from Canada to the U.S., Mukherjee writes, was "a movement away from the aloofness of expatriation, to the exuberance of immigration."

It is our own insecurity as a nation—our Sisyphus-like quest to protect that essential Canadianness—that has, for so long, prevented us from seeing the Canada that is right before our eyes. And it is because of this failure that many immigrants wear their Canadianness so tentatively, as if they landed here through compromise, chance and default, rather than being drawn here by an exciting, ongoing experiment in nation-building. In the absence of a uniquely Canadian immigration mythology, multiculturalism in Canada feels more accidental than essential—a demographic fluke rather than a true expression of who we are.

Ironically, it is those outside our borders who seem most able to appreciate Canada for what it has become, by accident or otherwise. In his recent book, *Global Soul*, Pico Iyer (who was raised in England by Indian parents, works in the U.S., and resides in Japan) identifies Toronto as a kind of city of the future. For him, "Hogtown" is nothing less than a hothouse global village where expat writers from around the world, freed from the confines of their ancestral homelands and unencumbered by American jingoism, are "creating visions for the post-national future." There is an essential restlessness in Canadian immigrant literature, Iyer observes, an urgency to the imaginings of elsewhere. This is the global condition, of course, but in Toronto, artists are finding a safe place to stay put and take a breath because this city, unlike so many others, "speaks to as many of our homes as possible."

Yet here in Canada, we aren't sure if Iyer's global village is really our own. Of course, we are reflexively proud of any Canadian writer who makes good internationally, but many of us are secretly still not quite sure whether Michael Ondaatje, Nino Ricci, Shyam Selvadurai, and Rohinton Mistry are telling real Canadian stories. How can these narratives of 1970s Bombay, 1920s Ceylon, or the ocean between Molise, Italy, and Toronto's "Little Italy" tell us as much about who we are as a narrative set in a Manitoba farmhouse?

And so, once again, we look to the past, to a time when our identities were purer, when our homelands stayed put. And yet what could be more Canadian than these stories of placelessness, exile and perennial homesickness? Surely the act of being caught between changing cultures—whether it is the colonialism of Nouvelle France, or the more-British-than-the-British airs of Colombo—speaks to an essentially Canadian experience. Yet, some-how, the search for home among Canada's global souls and the search for the soul of this most global nation seem unable to con-verge into a common national project, one that would provide both an identity for this country and a true home for all of its citizens.

It's not clear why this should be such a daunting challenge. Other countries, after all, face the great difficulty of having to rec-oncile a reality that no longer matches up to its own mythology. One thinks of the nation satirically depicted in Julian Barnes's *England, England*, so weighed down with its own idea of itself that it degenerates into a Brit-kitsch theme park, or worse, of China, reduced to selling Mao keychains in the shadow of Nike super-stores. In Canada, we have an eminently more hopeful problem: we don't yet have the shared mythology and icons to live up to our reality, so we take our great multicultural experiment for granted, even denounce it as a failure at the slightest provocation.

This is, of course, a vicious cycle. As long as immigrant his-tory and tradition are not embraced at the very centre of Canadian identity (and colourful displays of traditional dancing and drumming before APEC trade summits don't count), immigrants will always be haunted by the detachment of the expat, and that detachment will be reflected in the way immigrants choose to form communities and to make art. Likely these projects will be infused, as Mr. Bissoondath so rightly observes, with dreams of elsewhere, forever non-committal as to whether Canada is a true homeland.

If many Canadians feel a superficial connection to their chosen country, it is because they have never really been invited to go deeper—to enter the closed club of essential Canadianness still largely defined by the ups and downs of Anglo-French and East-West relations. Thinking people respond to half-hearted or fair-weather inclusion the only way that makes sense: by building and defending safe, comfortable enclaves.

The true flaw of multiculturalism is not that it encourages segregation, but that it helps disguise it by allowing our political elites to point to colourful displays of officially sponsored ethnicity as evidence that we, as a nation, have outgrown our colonial mindset. Multiculturalism is not "paying people to maintain their foreign roots," as its critics suggest, it is a payoff: paying ethnic groups to stay out of the way. By encouraging the creation of walled-off ethnic theme parks, the gatekeepers of Canadianness keep the competition occupied and protect their turf.

It needn't be so. Canada is the result of boats, not birthrights. Even rickety, rusty boats. Especially rickety, rusty boats. Our past is a collection of pasts; without this diversity, there is no Canada. This is it, right in front of us: the steady stream of immigrants who have chosen to come here and the people whose land it was before we arrived. There is no essential Canadianness that we have somehow misplaced, buried in our long-forgotten, glorious past. All that is there is Britain and France—more dreams of elsewhere.

But until we collectively embrace our shared experience as culture jumpers, we will be stuck with this reductive relationship to our history, one that shrinks us as a nation, rather than stretching the boundaries of our nationhood.

Fortunately, the possibilities for fusing another kind of identity from our collective pasts are both challenging and glorious. As Iyer observes, being home to millions of global souls gives our country an advantage immeasurable by productivity and foreign investment indexes: we are already the global village being promised to the rest of the world. But in order for this creativity to be liberated at last, our schools need to teach the stories of the Poles and Ukrainians who settled the Prairies, the Italians who constructed our cities, the Chinese who built the transcontinental railway, the black Loyalists who helped settle Nova Scotia and the Japanese who developed the West Coast fisheries. These stories should not be presented as syrupy morality plays about our open doors and compassionate hearts, however. They should be told the way they actually unfolded: as the history of a country that wanted to enjoy the benefits of cheap foreign labour without being infected by the corrosive influences of "alien" cultures.

Mr. Bissoondath believes knowing our history can bind us together as a nation, but it can also serve another, equally important function: it can help us understand why we are often so very far apart. If we are willing to look back honestly, we might find ways to move forward as a more united country, one with a fully evolved identity, expansive enough to include all Canadians. If we don't, we will never break down the segregation that now passes for multiculturalism or the binary bickering that passes for nation-building.

ARE WE A NATION OF INSTITUTIONS OR IDEAS?

Some commentators have taken to calling Canada a nation of institutions, not ideas. Is there a set of principles upon which Canada was founded and Confederation built? How have these principles evolved? Are they relevant to understanding and animating today's political culture and values?

THE UNFOUNDED COUNTRY

BY BARRY COOPER

JUST BECAUSE CANADA EXISTS doesn't mean that it was ever founded. In fact, the whole notion of founding a country is alien to Canadian experience. Founding is something undertaken by a Machiavellian new prince, but Canadian sovereignty has devolved historically from the very old British Crown. The Americans and the French, with their fancy republican ways, speak easily enough about their founding fathers—Washington, Madison, Robespierre, Marat, and all the rest. Canadians don't.

True, we use the same patriarchal language and speak of the Fathers of Confederation, but nobody talks about the fathers of Canada, which indicates clearly enough that Confederation was an episode in Canada's evolution, not a brand new beginning. A few intellectuals might indulge in loose talk about the Canadian founding, but they ought to know better.

Usually, the act of founding is accompanied by a heavy traffic in high-minded ideas intended to make the new citizens feel good about the violent things they are doing. Truths are held to be self-evident. The founders promise liberty, equality, and sisterhood, or peace, bread, and other people's land. None of that has ever happened in Canada, though political parties, such as the New Democrats or Reform, have staged founding events to haul themselves into existence.

Unfounded though Canada is, our early political life was not hostile to ideas. These were not expressions of grand new principles, but, as contemporary politicians would have said, embodiments of "well-known" ideas, well-known because they were part of a tradition the origins of which were discreetly shrouded in the mists of time. Chief among these ideas were the principles of parliamentary government and of liberalism. These remain important today. Indeed, many of our difficulties, as well as our successes, are a direct reflection of the extent to which we have maintained liberal and parliamentary government, or drifted away from it.

At the closing of the first session of the first Parliament of Upper Canada in 1792, Governor John Graves Simcoe reminded his advisers "that this province is singularly blest, not with a mutilated constitution, but with a constitution which has stood the test of experience, and which is the very image and transcript of that of Great Britain." These sentiments were recalled in the *British North America Act* of 1867—when Canada received "a Constitution similar in Principle to that of the United Kingdom"—and, in a more muted way, in the 1982 constitution as well.

In fact, parliamentary government in North America began long before the American Revolution. In its primitive form, elected assemblies could not control the executive. After the publication of Lord Durham's famous Report, the course towards responsible government and today's parliamentary institutions was set, at least in eastern Canada: the Crown is advised by a council that is supported in an assembly that in turn raises and spends money. Parliamentary government is finely balanced between executive decisiveness and the need for prudent and public justification of policy before the skeptical eyes of a "loyal opposition," which is also a government-in-waiting.

Responsible government—parliamentary government, properly speaking—came to the old colonies of British North America around the middle of the nineteenth century. On the Prairies, however, it was delayed "for the purposes of the Dominion" until 1930, when the provinces gained control over resource revenues. The timing could not have been worse. A decade of severe deflation, followed by the massive centralization of wartime, meant that political leaders in the West were deprived of the practical education in the ways of Parliament that their colleagues in the East had experienced for a least a generation before 1870.

In consequence, while liberalism in the West has been robust, it is also often extra-parliamentary. From the nineteenth-century agrarians to today's Reform party, populist liberalism has mounted a serious challenge to the conventions of Parliament. When sovereignty is thought to be vested in "the people" and not in the Crown, the implications for the cabinet, the executive, and the assembly are huge. Populist measures—the initiative, referendum, and recall, for example—are, in fact, incompatible with parliamentary government. You can have one or the other, but not both.

As a result, the populist liberalism of Canada's West has been a recipe for distress. Sometimes it has been dismissed as a reflection of the unwillingness of Parliament in Ottawa to respond to the interests of Westerners. From the National Policy of Sir John A. Macdonald to the National Energy Program of Pierre Trudeau, evidence to support this view is not hard to find. But more than interests are involved. Injured pride, not neglected interests, lies behind the ambivalence of many Westerners towards parliamentary government and Ottawa.

Pride matters. Indeed, human beings are especially proud when they rise above their interests, which is why the pride of

Westerners is especially insulted when the beneficiaries—Easterners for the most part—are so palpably ungrateful.

In so many ways, Quebec is a mirror image of the West. There "Ottawa" carries the same ambivalent symbolic charge, but for quite different reasons. In Quebec, the levers of parliamentary power have been energetically grasped, but diverted to distinctly non-liberal purposes.

It is useful to recall that, in Quebec, liberalism came ashore with the soldiers of General Wolfe in 1759. In those days, its most important element was freedom of religion, which opened the way for non–Roman Catholic, and often English-speaking, traders to settle in the newly acquired colony and to prosper. Once again, the effect of this infusion of liberal enterprise led to the recommendations of Lord Durham. But many French Canadians were less interested in individual liberty than in sheltering their community from the malign outside forces that the entrepreneurial English liberals seemed to represent. This explains why Durham's name is still mud in Quebec.

The same religious solidarity of the eighteenth-century resistance to liberalism could be detected in the writings of Abbé Lionel Groulx fifty years ago. With the massive and rapid secularization brought about by the Quiet Revolution, the words changed, but the music remained the same. The elegant Hegelian rhetoric of a sovereignist such as the late Fernand Dumont, for whom every distinct society achieves fulfillment and proper form as a state, and the claims in favour of "deep diversity" made on behalf of Quebec by a federalist such as Charles Taylor resonate with the same anti-liberal communitarian survivalism pioneered by François-Xavier Garneau a century and a half ago. Garneau's long poem, "Louise," and his multi-volume *Histoire du Canada*, were as much a *littérature de combat* as anything from the pens of contemporary Quebec nationalists, whether sovereignist or not. *Plus ça change...*

In fact, many things have changed since the days of Simcoe, Durham, and Macdonald, but the principles they espoused can still be detected without too much effort. And yet, pure parliamentary liberalism has never worked in Canada. All Canadians, and especially those in the immovable centre of the country, Ontario, should be grateful for the impurities supplied by the communitarian realities of Quebec and the extra-parliamentary populism of the West. These impurities provide colour and flavour to Canadian politics, the leaven that makes federalism work, even though they violate not a few of the explicit intentions of the Fathers of Confederation.

TOLERANCE AND ITS ENEMIES

BY BOB RAE

EIGHTY YEARS AGO, just as the First World War was ending, a book appeared in Ontario. It was titled *The Clash!: A Study in Nationalities*. Its author, a young student of Canadian history and politics, was one William Henry Moore. It must have sold well: my copy is from the fifth printing in six months.

The book was written in the midst of great tension both at home and abroad. The war had generated a political crisis at home: Borden's Union government had insisted on passing the *Military Service Act*. Laurier had refused to join the national coalition, and his Liberal party was reduced to a rump. In Ontario, the Tories passed a regulation under the *Education Act*—the now notorious Regulation 17—banning French as a language of instruction and insisting on the folly of "bi-lingual education."

The theme of *The Clash!* is the paradox of Canadian history itself. We pride ourselves on being a thoughtful, generous, tolerant people. Political bromides reinforce the image every day. The reality is a little different. At our best we have learned to appreciate harmony in diversity, but much of our story is about intolerance and conflict.

More than two hundred years ago, the British Parliament debated the *Quebec Act*. Two speeches stand out, the first from Sir Edward Thurlow, then Attorney General:

You ought to change those laws only which relate to the
French Sovereignty, and in their place substitute laws
which should relate to the new sovereign...but with
respect to all other laws, all other customs and institutions whatever, which are indifferent to the state of
subjects and sovereign, humanity, justice and wisdom
equally conspire to advise you to leave to the people just
as they were.

In this same debate Edmund Burke said, "I consider the right of
conquest so little, and the right of human nature so much, that the
former has little consideration with me."

The *Quebec Act*, the creative partnership between Baldwin and
Lafontaine, the Proclamation of 1763, the Confederation Debates,
the generosity of spirit exhibited by Laurier and Lester Pearson in
attempting to deal fairly with minorities: this is the line of partnership and tolerance.

Yet, our propensity for intolerance shows up as well:
Durham's disastrous, but fortunately short-lived, Report;
Macdonald's decision to hang Louis Riel; Ontario's move to
restrict the use of French in the early twentieth century; the isolationist appeals to race from a burgeoning Quebec nationalism;
the deeply conflicting emotions aroused by deep crises over conscription in two world wars; the increasingly sterile and fruitless
confrontations of the 1970s, 1980s, and 1990s, with the tragic slay-
ing of Pierre Laporte forever marking radical separatism with
deep and permanent dishonour: this is also our history.

The recognition of the identity of nationalities within Canada
and the concomitant spirit of partnership is about freedom itself.
The modern state can never be co-terminous with "the nation"
without a brutal exercise in ethnic cleansing. Our founding

principles are diversity and unity: Canada is a federation, not just a nation, and that says it all.

Thomas D'Arcy McGee, the great advocate of Confederation, once said, "Federalism is a great principle that speaks to the very foundations of human nature." One of Canada's great orators, McGee knew that a pure and simple ethnic or religious nationalism could not bring a lasting solution to the problems of the Ireland of his birth, a view that led to his assassination in 1868 at the hands of Fenian nationalists. Tens of thousands of deaths later, Irish discussions continue the effort to waken from a nightmare of remembered—sometimes real, sometimes exaggerated, sometimes imagined—grievance.

McGee was right about Ireland. He also was right about Canada. McGee understood that Canada's diversity required a different public philosophy from its colonial past.

In our wiser moments, we have listened to voices like Burke and McGee. Treaties have been signed with rights to both sides. Clear limits have been placed on what any temporary majority could do. From the very origins of these first encounters we have had to learn that rights can belong to groups as well as to individuals, and that pure and simple majority rule cannot be the only principle of civilized political community.

"Events stronger than advocacy; events stronger than men" (to borrow McGee's words) produced the drive to federal union. But it was not, on any terms, a drive to a unitary state. Quebec could best "be for itself" within a federal Canada.

Today there is great need for us to be clearer and more emphatic across the country on the benefits and meaning of the federalism that we have been building not just for 125 years, but, I would argue, since 1774 and the *Quebec Act*. There is a lot of misunderstanding with respect to the meaning and the essence of federalism in the province of Quebec, but there is an equal level of misunderstanding and misrepresentation in other parts of the country.

Those who argue that Canada is made up of ten provinces that must be treated exactly the same—a cookie-cutter approach to equality—are arguing in defiance of Canadian history. Such an approach may fit one person's theories of federalism, but we have seen the danger of governing in the name of a theory, whether it is Lord Durham's, Pierre Trudeau's or Preston Manning's.

Federalism takes different forms in different countries at different times. There is not one magic definition of federalism. There is not just one way in which one can be a federalist. There is not one, and only one, federalist constitution. There are a range of constitutional possibilities. Above all, in making constitutions, we should have respect for and knowledge of the institutions, the culture, the language and the history of our own country.

Those outside Quebec whose voices have rejected the notion of distinct society are ignoring an important part of Canadian history and Canadian reality. For generations, people outside Quebec have persisted in asking the typical media question, "What does Quebec want?" I think Quebec is now entitled to say, "Well, we have a pretty good idea of what we want. We told you what that was in Meech Lake. We've given you some sense of the direction we want to go in." There's clearly a strong majority of opinion in Quebec not in favour of separation, but certainly in favour of recognizing the particular quality of Quebec institutions. Now Quebec is entitled to say to English Canada, "What do you want?"

Whatever the results of the next referendum in Quebec—if there is one—certain common realities must be confronted. Political relations can always be improved, but a common currency and shared values clearly imply coordination and reciprocity, as they are doing in Europe.

These, in turn, will require common political institutions, such as Parliament and courts, with some powers independent of the member governments of the federation and common to all citizens. These common federal institutions can always be reformed. The appointed Senate will be abolished. Our relationship with the monarchy will be reassessed. Parliament itself can usefully change. But for all these changes, an underlying truth remains: the idea of Canada, a nation and civil society with a history of partnership and solidarity, remains as strong and vibrant as we care to make it.

POSTSCRIPT BY
BARRY COOPER

BOB RAE'S GUIDED TOUR through Canadian history points out many beautiful monuments, criticizes a few ugly episodes and discreetly avoids much that is ambiguous. It is both an edifying and a misleading experience. In two places I must take issue with him directly, and in a third encourage him to go further.

First is the contentious matter of Louis Riel. Rae is not alone in considering Riel's hanging to have been a big mistake. In 1999, a private member's bill was introduced to the House of Commons that declared Riel "wrongfully tried, convicted and executed." According to an Angus Reid poll undertaken at about the same time, 65 per cent of respondents would forgive him. This is a very bad idea.

There are two kinds of pardons available in Canadian law. The first, a free pardon, implies a person has been wrongly convicted. But Riel's trial was fair. He did, in fact, make war upon his sovereign. A free pardon is therefore out of the question. The second, an ordinary pardon, is possible, but would be purely symbolic. And what would it symbolize?

Riel was rightly convicted of high treason. In 1885, the Crown declined to accept the jury's recommendation of mercy. In fact, his nineteenth-century followers were treated with much more leniency than, for example, traitors were after the War of 1812, who were exiled and executed in substantially greater numbers. Mercy today would be an empty gesture because it could not expunge Riel's crime. Moreover, to pretend that Riel was anything other than a traitor or that justice was not carried out in 1885 would be the worst sort of historical revisionism. Like Stalin's removal of Trotsky from the official history of the Soviet Union, this idea belongs to the fictional world of George Orwell's "Ministry of Truth" in 1984. Louis Riel was by no means a "Father of Confederation." He was a traitor who was rightfully hanged. Cynical sentimentalism is not what the country needs today.

Second, there is poor Lord Durham. In my first article, I indicated that Canada has been informed from its beginnings in the aftermath of the American Revolution with two principles: liberalism and what soon came to be called the "well-known" principles of responsible or parliamentary government. After Confederation, responsible government was further modified by federalism. These are the enduring principles that will guide Canadians into the next century.

Liberalism means many things. In my first piece, I referred to Lord Durham and his splendid Report. Bob Rae referred to it as well, but alas, neglected to praise its many virtues. According to him, it was "disastrous, but fortunately short-lived." *Au contraire!* It was a splendid piece of work, and so filled with foresight that even today it informs Canadian political life at its best. To see why, we must understand Durham's liberalism on its own terms, and apart from what present-day liberals have become.

Lord Durham was a confident, strong, and spirited liberal. He knew liberalism was worth defending and he was eager to criticize its enemies. For over a century, the conventional reading of the Durham Report has praised the author for recommending responsible government, but criticized his proposal to assimilate French-speaking colonists. Indeed, in these days of official bilingualism and semi-official multiculturalism, this proposal seems intolerant and, because contemporary liberals can tolerate anything but intolerance, it looks illiberal as well. But Durham knew he had real enemies, which is why he was less suspicious of his friends than are present-day liberals.

Consider the circumstances in which Durham found himself. Following the Rebellion of 1837, he was faced with a "fatal feud" between the French- and English-speaking colonists of Lower Canada. He also had to consider dissatisfaction with British rule in the other colonies. Only by adapting to a common North American way of living could French-speakers enjoy genuine liberty. Thus did he advocate equality of opportunity and British constitutional practices. Thus, too, his liberalism: no religious cult, no clan, no tribe, no caste, no nation, no collective, no faction, and no king should usurp the right to legislate on behalf of others. That liberal principle endures in this country because it reflects the justifiable pride of individual citizens, whatever language they speak.

Existing practices, Durham was convinced, would ensure that "the great part" of French-speakers would remain "labourers in the employ of English capitalists," and so poor, dependent, jealous, and resentful. Generations of historians, writing in both French and English, have shown that Durham was not in error.

The French-speaking colonists, he said, did not wish to "remain stationary" but had been held back by a misguided policy that both permitted immigration of aggressive English-speaking entrepreneurs to Quebec and maintained the old seigneuries. Because the seigneuries could not easily be sold, the economic competitiveness of the French-speakers was reduced.

Durham was nevertheless lavish in his praise of the qualities of French Canadians. They were "amiable, virtuous, and contented" as well as "kindly, frugal, industrious, and honest," and blessed with "the language, the manners, and the institutions of a

great nation." And yet Durham did not characterize these qualities simply as virtues, but as "ancient virtues." They were not,
therefore, modern ones. Marxists, no doubt, would call them "pre-
capitalist" virtues.

Regardless of whether British policy was inspired by a good-
hearted desire to maintain the noble but vanishing life of the
ancien régime or by prejudice against the Catholic and French
inhabitants of the colony, the result was identical: the English-
speaking minority prospered and the majority of French
speakers did not. It was a recipe for strife. It was also the reason
why colonists on both sides argued in terms of "race." That is,
the English speakers wished to protect their group privileges,
and the French speakers challenged them on the same grounds.
By promoting individuals, Durham was no ally of the dominant
English speakers, but the best friend of the French speakers of
Lower Canada.

He was also perhaps the first to notice the *mauvaise foi* of
nationalist rhetoric. It was designed not to resist assimilation to
liberal ways but to protest the exclusion of French speakers from
the prosperous society of English-speaking merchants. Durham
therefore opposed legal protection for a "distinct society" in
Lower Canada. In his opinion, the artificial preservation of a society of ancient virtue, like the "separate but equal" institutions of
the American South, would violate his liberal faith in equality of
opportunity. Like the contemporary political philosopher
Michael Oakeshott, Lord Durham saw the legisled prolonga-
tion of ancient virtue as leading to the creation of an "association
of invalids."

Much like the sovereignists today, the Patriote rebels of 1837
were not dedicated to preserving the ancient virtues and cultural
traditions of their ethnic garrison. Although they invoked nation-

alist sentiments to justify their opposition, their appeal to the back-
ward, pre-modern, and pre-liberal habitants was intended to gain
electoral support—a thoroughly modern and liberal objective—in
order to effect liberal reforms against the discriminatory laws supported by the English-speaking faction. The Patriotes were moved
by modern ambition, not nostalgia for ancient virtues. They
sought power through institutional reform, not salvation through
piety and fidelity to an exclusive ecclesiastical society.

In other words, by the 1830s, the French-speaking population
of Lower Canada had learned how to operate in a British parliamentary regime—something they had not known at the conquest
two generations earlier. It is worth recalling that four of the
Patriotes of 1837 (Lafontaine, Morin, Cartier, and Taché) went on
to become prime ministers of the United Provinces of Canada.
These men were politically assimilated. They were solid liberals,
which is why, in 1837, they found discrimination on the grounds of
intolerable ethnicity.

Likewise, today's sovereignists—no less than today's federalists—share liberal political habits, customs, and manners. This is
why the sovereignists become so irritated when their opponents
criticize their *pure laine* rhetoric as ethnocentric, and worse. And
yet, like the Patriotes of 1837, they do make archaic and anti liberal
appeals against, for example, "money and the ethnic vote," to use
the unforgettable phrase of Jacques Parizeau.

In recommending equal opportunity, Durham's message was
simple: wherever ethnic, linguistic, or religious differences are
politically institutionalized, there one finds injustice. This liberal
principle has endured in Canada because it guarantees the dignity
of all citizens, whatever language they speak. That is what makes
Lord Durham such a great liberal, and why his Report remains an
enduring statement of Canadian liberalism.

The great challenge for liberals today stems from a misguided nostalgia for community. There are many social ills around, from poverty, violence, and drug addiction on native reserves to homophobia, gender discrimination, and the mistreatment of visible minorities. As a remedy, liberals infected with communitarian sentiments seek to establish forms of collective representation based on gender, race, ethnicity, culture, sexual orientation, and so forth.

Assuming their good intentions, these "command liberals," as they have been called, are open to the same criticisms that Durham levelled at the British government in 1839. In contemporary language, there are no non-arbitrary decision rules by which to assign individuals to specific collectivities. Thus, for example, is an Ungava Cree an aboriginal or a Quebecer? And what of minorities within minorities? Should a disabled, lesbian Cree be protected against able-bodied, non-lesbian Cree, and both protected against the non-Cree Quebecers who are protected against non-Quebecers? The problem is obvious: there is no a priori way to determine which substantive or cultural cleavage is most important. Accordingly, discussion degenerates into a high-decibel dialogue of the deaf, a collection "of socially malcontent anarchist poets," as one observer put it.

In the example of a disabled, lesbian Cree, the only non-arbitrary way to decide what substantive minority culture counts for the individual is to leave it up to her. But then the logic for privileging any group disappears as well, and that means the state has an obligation to be neutral, which is what liberals such as Durham maintained all along.

In the context of Durham's arguments rightly understood, Rae was correct to observe that "Canada is a federation, not just a nation, and that says it all." It doesn't quite say it all, but it says a great deal: we are a "political nation," to use Cartier's formula in the Confederation Debates, and we are a federation.

It is not, however, "cookie-cutter" federalism, as Mr. Rae suggests, to treat the provinces as formally equal. Acknowledging the reality of equal provinces has become a political necessity, and largely for the liberal reasons that Durham made plain as day in his Report. A liberal society is based on variety and, indeed, requires variety for its survival. Federalism, a mode of governance that enhances liberal "experiments in living," is the institutional expression of variety concentrated.

Today, few dispute that Quebec is more distinct from Prince Edward Island than Saskatchewan is from Manitoba, but the two Prairie provinces are not cookie cut-outs either. Here is where the former premier of Canada's most populous province is too timid in his understanding of what federalism will do for diversity in Canada.

There may be good reasons for Quebec to take pride in its language laws, whatever English-speakers in British Columbia might think. By the same token, there is no good reason why Saskatchewan should not take pride in its own gun laws, whatever the good burghers of Montreal might think. Likewise, Alberta can take pride in its own tax, pension, and health laws despite the disapproval of the *bien pensants* of Toronto or of bureaucrats in Ottawa.

Federalism is meant to be experimental and competitive. It encourages the same variety that both strengthens the foundations of liberal society and gives it full expression. Quebec's language laws, no less than the existence of Nunavut, are experiments. In both places, citizens are better able to use local or regional government for their own purposes, to organize their common life without being intimidated by a remote and massive central government and to take pride in their achievements. Federalism encourages these liberal virtues by promoting government that is not only responsible but also responsive.

In this new millennium, Canadians can be sure that new political necessities will ensure new political experiments. They can be confident that the competitive principles of liberalism and federalism will be equal to the challenge.

POSTSCRIPT BY
BOB RAE

CANADA IS A FEDERATION. This may seem an exceedingly boring and obvious statement. But like many truisms, it is true. Canada cannot be understood as a unitary state, or as a country that can be run from the centre.

Canada's first separatist government was not from Quebec, but from Nova Scotia. Joseph Howe's pulverizing election victory over Charles Tupper in 1868 was a referendum on a single issue, Confederation. The provincial government spent its first year petitioning the British Colonial Secretary to let Nova Scotia out of the 1867 deal. The request was refused in no uncertain terms:

> Vast obligations, political and commercial, have already
> been contracted on the faith of a measure so long
> discussed and so solemnly adopted...the Queen's
> government feel that they would not be warranted in
> advising the reversal of a great measure of state, attended
> by so many extensive consequences already in operation.

Nova Scotia accepted the decision. *Force majeure* spoke. The tide of history swept aside local claims and regional voices. But this did not end the frustration. A key consequence of Macdonald's National Policy was to tie the Atlantic provinces increasingly to central Canada. Whether a different arrangement would have changed the pattern of economic development in the Maritimes is a matter of deep disagreement. What is important is that the feeling of regional resentment against the centre was embedded in the country from the very beginning.

While Joseph Howe and his friends were fighting a losing battle, Louis Riel was attempting to establish a distinct society on the banks of the Red River to the west. Once again, the Macdonald administration, which had as profound a centralizing bent as any in Canadian history until the advent of Pierre Elliott Trudeau, went to great lengths to assert federal power and discipline. The conflict eventually led to rebellion and Riel's death at the hands of an executioner. Macdonald's decision to hang Riel had more than one fateful result. Quebec was incensed. Laurier was empowered. The Tories were long associated with more than just racial intolerance; they were also linked with the use of the long arm of central power to enforce conformity and Ottawa's supremacy. My point about Riel is not that we should rewrite history. It is that Macdonald's decision to let him hang had profound consequences.

The central ambiguity of Confederation itself was that to some Quebecers it could only be swallowed because it broke the nearly thirty-year yoke of the centralized Province of Canada, while to Macdonald himself it provided for clear pre-eminence from Ottawa. Lord Durham, twenty-five years earlier, had hoped that assimilation and majority rule would eventually asphyxiate French-Canadian nationalism. Of course they did no such thing. The distinct identity of French Canada was fiercely protected in the years after 1840.

While Rouges like Laurier opposed Confederation, they soon saw it as inevitable, and, ultimately, an advantage for Quebec. Ironically, it was Sir John A.'s old law partner, a determined Grit by the name of Oliver Mowat, who championed provincial rights against the centralizing Macdonald. Mowat managed to convince the British Law Lords, who oversaw our constitutional development, that provinces mattered, that they were not local creatures of the national government but had sovereign power in their own way. Canada's federalism was not simply the product of decisions taken at Charlottetown. It has constantly evolved, with competing periods of centralization and devolution.

The immigrant families who went West from central Canada and Europe quickly created provinces with a culture different from "the East." This political style was more egalitarian, less deferential, and ultimately more radical than anything seen at the centre. The existence of high tariffs and Imperial preference, both confirmed in the Conservative victory over Laurier in 1911, gave permanent fuel to the sense among Western farmers that they were subsidizing Ontario and Quebec manufacturers and being denied free and fair access to the lucrative American market. Their own prices were set by Eastern cartels. Western radicalism was born of this sense of unfairness. It fuelled the Winnipeg General Strike of 1919, the election of dozens of Progressive MPs in the election of 1921, and a growing sense that the centre just wasn't listening.

The election of Social Credit in Alberta and the CCF in Saskatchewan clearly sent the message that a different sense of politics was at work. The conflicts with the feds were partly about money and resources. They were also, in good measure, about values. Alberta's Aberhart and Manning quarrelled with Ottawa about the regulation of the press, Saskatchewan's Tommy Douglas about the insurance industry and health care. Their political popularity was reinforced by their willingness to stand up to the world of Eastern Fat Cats and Bureaucrats. Farmers organized themselves against the grain interests of Winnipeg, Chicago, and Toronto; provincial economies grew steadily as resources increased in value and importance. The country was into full-fledged "province building" and Western pride.

The last thirty years have only seen a deepening of these historic tensions. Mythology would have it that Mr. Diefenbaker's triumphant election in 1958 was cut short by a conspiracy of the Eastern establishment. Like Joe Clark's short-lived victory twenty years later, a more objective view would clearly see it as more a case of suicide than of manslaughter. But the myth was fuelled.

The Pearson administration's preoccupation with the partnership between English and French received short shrift in the West. Alberta's premier, Ernest Manning, sent Mr. Pearson a sharp letter on the formation of the Royal Commission on Bilingualism and Biculturalism in which he made it clear that the commission did not reflect his vision of the country. But no administration galvanized Western opinion as sharply as Mr. Trudeau's. Not only was he seen as mesmerized by Quebec's political agenda, but his views of resource management, energy pricing, and constitutional change guaranteed opposition victories across the West just as surely as Macdonald's decision on Riel (and Borden's on conscription) guaranteed the election of Liberals in Quebec for generations.

If Mr. Trudeau did as much as anyone to galvanize regional grievance, Mr. Mulroney did his best to placate it. The irony is that Mulroney's legacy was rewarded by the Reform party of Preston Manning repeating the sweep of the Progressives, Social Credit, and the CCF in the years after the First and Second World Wars. Manning's quest for the Triple-E Senate and his berating of central Canada has left him with the enduring image of a regional spokesman. This has tainted Reform east of Manitoba.

The final irony is that the advent of free trade and the steady erosion of the fiscal strength of the federal government has fuelled regional resentment in Ontario itself. Dean Acheson once said of Great Britain that it had lost an empire and was looking for a role. The same could now be said of Ontario. With the abandonment of the National Energy Program, the signing of the NAFTA, and the decision to discriminate against Ontario in fiscal transfers, Ottawa created an inevitable dynamic: those who are treated as regions will react in a regional fashion.

Yet the centre needs a continuing capacity to act for the whole country. The persistence of resentments of every kind from one corner of Canada to another is the least attractive feature of our national character. There is no avoiding resentments: the challenge is to put them in perspective. To borrow from the rabbi's ancient three questions, we must be for ourselves, but not exclusively. The great Canadian radical William Lyon Mackenzie put it best:

> This then is politics. That part of our duty which
> teaches us to study the welfare of our whole country,
> and not to rest satisfied altho' our own household is
> well off when our neighbours are in difficulty and dan-
> ger. The honest politician is he who gives all he can and
> means to promote the public good, whose charity
> begins at home but does not end there. The man who
> says he is no politician is either ignorant of what he is
> saying or a contemptible selfish creature, unworthy of
> the country or community of which he is a part.

The issue of the kind of country we want to be is not just about English and French Canada, although it certainly must include that at its centre. The encounter between European and native has created its own tension in Canada, as profound as the encounters in all the Americas, in South Africa, and in Australia. The issue is about the importance of identity, the challenge of recognizing the otherness of others without giving in to the tyranny of differences, both large and small.

Successive generations have at one and the same time attempted to obliterate, conquer, convert, ignore, and romanticize the Canadians who occupied the continent first. The debate around the Nisga'a Treaty shows that the divide is far from over: a large number of Canadians reject the notion of native self-government. The "regional government" of Nunavut is not exclusively based on the Inuit people. But there is no denying the power of its claim to a specific cultural identity, as well as its profound link to its geography.

Is the country, then, just a "community of communities," a loose affiliation of regions, nations, provinces held together by habit and imagined grievance? The simple answer is no, of course not. Deciding to make a country was a deliberate decision in 1867. Citizenship matters, and so does the kind of governance we choose. As Canadians, we expected a strong degree of leadership from Macdonald and Laurier. We even accepted it from King. After the Second World War, right up to Pearson, we accepted the federal government's lead on building the key elements of the welfare state. Opinion overwhelmingly accepted the patriation of the Constitution and the Charter of Rights and Freedoms.

We may not have achieved a deep constitutional consensus on native self-government, Quebec's distinctiveness, or Senate reform, but that is no reason to give up on Canada. Nation-states and sovereignty will matter less in the twenty-first century. New international understandings about governance will be crucial. Local and regional governments will also matter more. But unless there is strong coordination, common purpose and shared citizenship, Canadians will rightly feel cheated of what they deserve. We have succeeded so far because we have been international in our focus, federal in our character and tolerant in our temperament. These will also be the keys to our success in the future.

WHERE HAVE ALL THE HEROES GONE?

Canada is largely ambivalent about its heroes, especially when compared with the mythology-rich United States. What are the origins of this predisposition? Has Canada suffered from its unwillingness to create national heroes? Or is our aversion to celebrating heroes and heroism quintessentially Canadian?

NO IDOL INDUSTRY HERE

BY CHARLOTTE GRAY

CANADA DOESN'T DO HEROES WELL. Look at our paper money for evidence of the scarcity of national symbols. Until recently, our bills featured prime ministers and birds in their natural terrain—emblematic of the only two brands of psychological glue that bind Canada together: political culture and love of landscape.

Of course, there is the Queen, too, with her Mona Lisa smile gleaming out from the hallmarked paper. But the monarchy has always been included on Canadian money—a remnant of our colonial past. If she weren't part of the family furniture, Elizabeth II would have been dropped years ago.

Other countries have liberators, scientists, authors, saints, war heroes—outstanding figures from the past who are supposed to represent the nation's greatness. We had the loon on our twenty-dollar bill and William Lyon Mackenzie King on our fifty-dollar bill. King, prime minister for twenty-two years, may have been one of our better leaders (number one out of twenty on a recent ranking), but he is hardly the figure to make Canadian bosoms swell with national pride.

Why are we so hero-poor? At one level, the answers to this question are embedded in the nature of Canada itself. We live in a country that has a weak national culture and strong regional identities. As historian Daniel Francis pointed out in *National*

Dreams: Myth, Memory and Canadian History: "In Canada, heroic figures have tended to emerge from the regions or from minority struggles against the status quo. By and large, they are sticks used by one part of the community to beat one another."

Louis Riel is a hero to Métis and francophones, and a mad troublemaker to anglophones. Even national figures are enmeshed in regional rivalries: Pierre Trudeau is the darling of Toronto's Liberal elite and a menace to Quebec nationalists and Alberta oilmen.

The majority of Canadians have been in the country for only two or three generations. Most of the first European arrivals carry far too much baggage. How can we glorify explorers like Jacques Cartier when they treated the First Nations as savages? Or military heroes like Generals Wolfe and Montcalm when they fought each other? Finding common ground for homegrown heroes is a challenge. Countries with homogenous populations and histories stretching back beyond the printed word can pickle their heroes in the sweet vinegar of centuries.

Easy for the Brits to accept Boadicea as a heroine, or for the French to revere the memory of Jeanne d'Arc: the mists of history have obscured Boadicea's murderous reputation and Jeanne d'Arc's psychiatric problems. Any women in Canadian history must stand much more brutal scrutiny, and measure up to 1990s values. So Susanna Moodie, whose *Roughing It in the Bush* is a vivid and gripping record of nineteenth-century pioneer life, fails as a hero because she expressed the snooty disdain of her class towards Irish immigrants. And Nellie McClung, the Western novelist who in the early years of this century fought for female suffrage, factory safety legislation, and women's rights, doesn't cut it for contemporary feminists because she glorified the traditional family.

Most countries choose individuals with larger-than-life qualities to mythologize: extraordinary imagination, against-the-odds bravery, brilliant creativity. There are colourful characters in our collective past who embody such qualities—think of Sir Sandford Fleming, inventor of Standard Time; Dr. Frederick Banting, co-discoverer of insulin; the fighter pilot Billy Bishop. Why aren't they on our money, instead of stuffy old Mackenzie King?

Fleming has never found an enthusiastic biographer, and Banting and Bishop are too damn controversial for Canada. Neither displayed the humility that is the first requisite of Canadian heroism. Prime Minister King, on the other hand, is respected (by those who respect him) for qualities that are seen as quintessentially Canadian—his skill at compromise, his success in keeping the country unified. "He was an unheroic leader," suggests historian Norman Hillmer, "who understood the contradictions of an unheroic country."

So we do heroes badly. Moreover, we do hero worship really badly. The United States has an idol industry for most of the founding fathers, plus a whole military-industrial complex for the Kennedys. British academics and writers churn out books on Churchill (and there is a blossoming Thatcher industry). France has myth-creation factories for both Napoleon Bonaparte and Charles de Gaulle. Each of these national heroes has sparked several million feet of film and a gazillion written pages (over fifteen thousand books on Napoleon and still counting).

It is not only national leaders who are celebrated in these countries: university library shelves groan with mega-bios and unpublished theses on Rockefeller, the American robber baron; Florence Nightingale, the autocratic Englishwoman who revolutionized nursing; or the French intellectual, Jean-Paul Sartre. Each of these characters incarnates a trait of which their country is proud: American industry, British guts, French brains.

But anti-heroes, such as Mackenzie King, don't spark such exuberant hero worship. Most Canadians are more interested in King's weird side—his interest in spiritualism and his penchant for table-tapping—than in his determination to strengthen Canadian independence or his intuitive grasp of how to make Canadians feel comfortable. In a fragmented country such as Canada, successful leaders embody modest virtues. But biographers looking for titans aren't interested in modest virtues. Cultural consumers only embrace these virtues when they are accompanied by extraordinary athletic prowess (come in, number 99) or teeth-gritting tragedy (Terry Fox).

There have been attempts to establish a pantheon of heroes—iconic reflections of our past and our psyche. In the early years of this century, when we were still suffused with the Victorian assumption that bearded patriarchs made the best heroes, the Toronto publisher George Morang commissioned a series of volumes under the title *Makers of Canada*. The "makers" in this twenty-volume collection, published between 1908 and 1911, were all men, all either French- or English-speaking, and almost all involved in public life, as governors, politicians, and premiers. There were three fur traders, but no entrepreneurs until the late addition of Sir William Van Horne, president of the Canadian Pacific Railway. There was not a single scholar, writer, artist, scientist, or athlete.

Mr. Morang's reverential volumes never caught the public imagination. They were out of step with the emerging Canadian sensibility. Their view of history was too restricted, and their style too prissy, for a young country hurtling towards a multicultural future.

The qualities that are celebrated in our national life today are collective virtues—the bravery of our peacekeepers, the compassion of all Canadians for Manitoba's flood victims. Our best-known artists are the Group of Seven. When writers want to pump some adrenaline into our past or present, they capture groups rather than individuals. Pierre Berton wrote about the whole ruling class of Sir John A.'s day when he penned *The Last Spike*. Peter Newman has described the raw ambition and acquisitive urges of the business establishment as the twentieth century has unfolded. The heroes of other nations are usually fiercely individualistic—but individualism has never been celebrated in Canada. It is not a useful quality for a loose federation perched on a magnificent and inhospitable landscape—a nation that sees survival as a collective enterprise.

WE'D RATHER BE CLARK KENT

BY PETER C. NEWMAN

HEROES REFLECT THE NATIONS that anoint them, and Canada is no exception. To the Americans, contemporary heroes tend to be androgynous, retroactive virgins, such as Ally McBeal, gum-chewing batters, such as Mark McGwire, or Monica Lewinsky, immortalized by her kneel-and-duck love life. Historically, the Yanks have benefited from the hero factory run by Walt Disney, who made demigods out of such frontier reprobates as Davy Crockett and Francis Marion, better known as "the swamp fox."

I have long argued that Canadian heroes—the few who have retained that state of grace—share one essential qualification: they're dead.

In our peculiar way, we do not salute living heroes, even when they deserve to be recognized, because that hints of boasting. This country is fuelled by envy and deference, qualities that rank hero-ism as an emotional extravagance reserved for Italian tenors and one-album country-and-western singers. If God had meant us to be heroic, he wouldn't have made us Canadians. This is the only country on earth whose citizens dream of being Clark Kent instead of Superman.

A good example is our reticence in decorating our military heroes. Ottawa has actually struck three Canadian medals for bravery—our own versions of the Victoria Cross, the Star of

Military Valour, and the Medal of Military Valour—but none has ever been awarded.

From the beginning of Canadian history, there have been some curious lapses in our choices. The St. Malo navigator Jacques Cartier is credited with Canada's "discovery" and is widely hailed, but John Cabot, that silk-clad Venetian dandy who had immigrated to England, made his landfall in Newfoundland or Cape Breton thirty-seven years earlier. Until the recent celebration of the anniversary of his voyage, the only memorials to Cabot were the scenic trail looping northern Cape Breton Island and the plaque on a drafty baronial tower on Signal Hill in St. John's, better known as the location of Guglielmo Marconi's earliest transatlantic signal transmission. If Cabot had only landed in what is now the United States, he would have been as famous as Christopher Columbus. (The Americans celebrate the befuddled Spanish navigator as their discoverer, though he didn't even sight North America's coastline and mistook Haiti for Japan.)

James Wolfe, Louis-Joseph de Montcalm and Isaac Brock were more appropriate Canadian heroes, since they died in battles without knowing their outcomes. And the memory of our most daring pirate, Antoine Laumet de Lamothe Cadillac, the privateer and fur trader who flourished in Quebec in 1691 and later founded Detroit, is perpetuated only by General Motors.

Except for Louis Riel, few of our deities have personified ideals central to their time and place. Riel belongs to a category all his own. He became Canada's presiding martyr by refusing, at his trial for high treason, to hide behind a justified plea of insanity that might have saved his life. He thus personified the quintessential Canadian hero: a deluded mystic who died prematurely by pretending to be sane.

There is little consensus on the nature of Canadian heroes, except that they're not politicians. We do not even officially mark the anniversary of our founding father, Sir John A. Macdonald, but celebrate instead Queen Victoria's birthday—long after it has been forgotten in the mother country. Of the modern crop, Pierre Trudeau, who most closely approached heroic status when he first boogied onto the scene in 1968, was quickly revealed as having an icicle for a heart, and was defeated in the 1979 election. By who? That's right—Joe Clark.

No Canadian politician ever lost his heroic aura faster than Brian Mulroney—the man with the Gucci smile—who harvested more votes than Trudeau ever did, when he swept the nation in 1984. Within months, Mulroney was being blamed for every sparrow that fell from the sky, while mothers were using his name as a threat to force their kids to eat spinach.

A rare exemption to our anti-hero worship is the Group of Seven, those determined hikers who glorified Ontario cottage country by turning it into derivative landscapes. (Most Canadians assume the Group of Seven was fronted by Tom Thomson—an authentic Canadian hero because he drowned under mysterious circumstances at the height of his fame. In fact, Thomson died three years before the Group was formed.)

Our anti-hero attitude extends even to our entertainers. If they're successful, they can't be real. Anne Murray, one of our first world-class popular singing stars, received this backhanded tribute from the music critic Larry LeBlanc in *Saturday Night* magazine: "If you close your eyes, and think of a naked Anne Murray, parts of her always come up airbrushed."

The most conspicuously heroic Canadian of recent times was, of course, Terry Fox, the young British Columbia athlete ravaged by cancer, who, in 1981, hobbled halfway between our coasts, before he collapsed. His heroic stature was confirmed when he was pinned with the Order of Canada on his deathbed. (What's-his-name, who followed Fox's path while suffering from the same affliction, actually completed his trek and raised millions for cancer research. But Steve Fonyo lived to tell the tale and has since been relegated to obscurity so chilling that he has felt compelled to commit a series of misdemeanours just to stay in print.)

Similarly, no one made much fuss about Dr. Norman Bethune until 1939, when he was sanctified in his heroic status by dying from neglecting a cut finger after operating on an infected patient as a member of Mao Tse-tung's Communist forces. (Wayne Gretzky retains his heroic stature only because he saw what was coming, and left the country.)

At another level, Canadians did not celebrate ambassador Ken Taylor's heroism in smuggling six U.S. diplomats out of the Ayatollah's reach during the American-Persian confrontation. Ottawa exacted revenge on the unconventional diplomat, who broke the rules when he took a risk on behalf of freedom, by refusing to offer him an appropriately senior posting following his stint as consul-general in New York, thus forcing his resignation.

One of the few Canadians who took advantage of how shabbily we treat our living heroes was Marshall McLuhan, who richly earned iconic status. He maintained his poise amid the customary slaughter dished out to our most thoughtful writers by the butchers who pass for book reviewers in these frosty latitudes (while becoming the *dahling* of New York's literati). But it didn't bother him. "I experience a great deal of liberty here in Canada," McLuhan once told me. "I wouldn't get that in the States, because I'm taken quite seriously there. The fact that Canadians don't take me seriously is a huge advantage. It makes me a free man."

McLuhan was wise enough to realize that being a hero in Canada is an existential state with a shorter shelf life than boysenberry yogurt. We have little talent for excess and no patience with anyone who believes that heroism is worth achieving, except perhaps by inadvertence. There is a vague but valid link between our heroes and our weather, which remains Canada's most essential reality. Our frigid climate reflects the selectivity of how we pick our heroes: many are cold, but few are frozen.

POSTSCRIPT BY
CHARLOTTE GRAY

I SUFFER FROM A VERY Canadian syndrome: TGIH.

What is TGIH? Well, let me explain it this way. Living here, I often suffer acute hero envy. Why can't Canada produce a brilliant literary bad boy such as Jay McInerney, or a steely-minded, successful politician such as Margaret Thatcher, or an outrageous sports personality such as Dennis Rodman? Why don't we spawn a few larger-than-life characters who bend the rules to fit them rather than shaping their own behaviour to the norm?

But then I leave Canada, perhaps to spend a few days on the turf of one of these braggadocio characters. On my return to Canadian soil, I am overwhelmed by TGIH. Thank God I'm Home, in a country where bully-boy tactics are not celebrated and civility is the norm. A country where we put dead and forgotten prime ministers, such as Robert Borden, on our banknotes, rather than kings and conquerors. The political and military heroes of other countries are celebrated for their fierce individualism, insensitivity to other points of view, and driving determination. But these are not Canadian qualities. Canada is not a militaristic nation.

We admire other virtues. Our public discourse is rarely characterized by Sturm und Drang and when presented with a silver lining, we instinctively look for the clouds. I don't care if people elsewhere jeer at Canada for being a decaffeinated version of the States. They can keep their Supermen and Superwomen, who exhibit a Darwinian selfishness in their teeth-gritting determination to survive. I breathe a sigh of relief that I am back in the land

of Clark Kent virtues—modesty, respect for others, a certain dif-
fidence, and a well-developed sense of the ridiculous. And a steady
ability to work with others for the common good.

Clark Kent virtues are not the stuff of conventional heroism.
They do not trigger the emotional extravagance that hero factories require to lubricate their output. Our most successful and
longest-serving prime minister, William Lyon Mackenzie King,
has generated fewer than a hundred biographies and books. A
dumpy little pragmatist who shunned photographers, King could
not have been less inspiring. Yet for over twenty years he rose bril-
liantly to the test that faces every Canadian prime minister, and
which most of his successors have failed: he kept a nation riven
with regional and linguistic tensions united. He was skilled in that
most Canadian of arts: compromise. More colourful (and almost
as long-serving) Canadian political leaders, such as Sir John A.
Macdonald and Pierre Trudeau, have a few thousand more pages
devoted to their wit, visions, long hair, and personal idiosyncrasies.
But neither enjoys the avalanche of celebratory biographies
inspired elsewhere by political leaders who radiate sex appeal
(John Kennedy) or national machismo (Winston Churchill).

These days, we have to make the distinction between celebrity
and heroism. Magazines such as *People, Talk,* or *Hello* smother the
super-rich, super-thin, and super-cool with indiscriminate syco-
phancy. They make money and glamour (or, in the case of people
like Pete Doherty or Mel Gibson, attitude and a bad haircut) seem
enough to guarantee you a place in the Hall of Fame. But this is
ephemeral celebrity, not long-term heroism. Heroes touch people's hearts not by appearance or achievement alone, but by less
tangible qualities—their strength of personality, perhaps, or the
way they capture in themselves the qualities that a nation believes
it represents. Some heroes are, in the words of my counterpart

Peter Newman, "go-getters who turn individual into collective history." But not all of them.

Newman has suggested that the one essential characteristic of all Canadian heroes is that they are dead. He argues that if a living Canadian laid claim to hero status, the rest of us would dismiss him or her as a boaster. As a nation, he states, we are "fuelled by envy." (The Japanese, who are similar to Canadians in that they attach more importance to collective than individual achievements, admit to the same sour-grapes behaviour. Citizens of the second most powerful nation in the world deplore their own tendency to cut down "tall poppies," as they call anybody with the nerve to stick his or her head above the crowd.) I would argue that Newman is using a borrowed and outdated definition of heroism, since his examples of heroes are European, pre-twentieth-century soldiers and explorers who displayed against-the-odds bravery in the service of some national ideal. That kind of physical bravery is passé in the age of microchip empires and dissolving national borders. Its only current manifestation is probably in the nerves-of-steel takeover duels between our contemporary titans of capitalism tracked by Newman himself in his chronicles of the Canadian business establishment. Head-to-head battles between the rich and powerful make amusing reading, but selflessness and national pride play no role in corporate slugfests.

It is true that Canada is not a land of alpha males. Of course, this exasperates the likes of Conrad Black, men who revel in confrontation. But look what we produce instead! Millennial Canada is a breeding ground for alpha females. Think of Céline Dion, Shania Twain, Diana Krall, Silken Laumann, or Ann-Marie MacDonald. Some of these talented women will morph into heroes by proving they have staying power in the public imagination.

There is a Canadian appetite for people who symbolize our nation, and for occasions to celebrate our pride in Canada. It is impossible to forget the national exuberance sparked by Expo 67, or the coast-to-coast whoop of delight when Donovan Bailey became the fastest man on earth in 1994. When the Millennium Partnership Project offered to help fund projects that would celebrate Canada's past achievements and individuals of note, it was inundated with applications. Two of the projects funded were a wooden sculpture of Tecumseh, the valiant Shawnee chief who fought for the British in 1812, and a national tour of a bronze maquette representing the five sturdy women who fought the Persons Case in 1929. A full-size version of the statue was unveiled on Parliament Hill in the year 2000.

I don't agree with Newman that heroes cannot be manufactured. History has always been written by the winners' spin doctors. If there has been a shortage of heroes in Canada, it is because we have lacked enough spin doctors. We certainly have enough victories in our past. So the challenge, for those who want to feed Canada's appetite for heroes, is to redefine heroism. Who are we, and what kind of heroes do we want? Who are the individuals, alive or dead, who typify the best aspects of Canada, a tolerant, successful, and unpretentious society with a sense of humour and a remarkable collective ability both to promote change and adapt to it? Just because our virtues are modest and anti-heroic doesn't mean that we have to celebrate wimps. Our characteristics throw up different kinds of heroes. Once you start matching Canadian qualities to Canadian achievers, you quickly realize that there is plenty of material to work with:

- Collective strength. A nation that is itself a collective balancing act is a high-wire act that works. What could be a better symbol than the Cirque du Soleil, a colourful, gasp-making acrobatic ballet that works without words? Performers swing through the air, use each other as counterweights, balance each other's needs—all without speaking. Just like the Canadian federation: geographical, gender, linguistic balance.

- Quiet competence. In international affairs, there have always been unassuming, brainy Canadians whose objective was a better world. They include John Humphrey, who drafted the Universal Declaration of Human Rights in 1948, and Prime Minister Lester Pearson, who developed the idea of a peace-keeping force. But one unsung hero is Louis Rasminsky (1908–1998), the soft-spoken, charming and gifted economist who was the *éminence grise* at the 1944 Bretton Woods conference. Having observed the monetary chaos of the 1930s and 1940s, he quietly designed the International Monetary Fund, which stabilized the global financial system so that countries, large and small, could prosper and grow in the postwar period. Because he was Canadian, he never took credit. Because Bretton Woods is in New Hampshire, the Americans got it.

- Respect for the land. Canadians have raped and pillaged their landscape as energetically as anyone, but since pre-Confederation days there have also been ecological champions—native and immigrant. Nineteenth-century author Catharine Parr Traill was among the first to realize the dangers of environmental destruction. While Walt Whitman was still waxing lyrical, she was on her hands and knees digging up ferns and identifying vanishing botanical species. A Rachel Carson before her time, until now she has been a prophet unrecognized in her own country...very Canadian.

- Common decency. No nation has a monopoly on this quality, but various Canadians have elevated it into a governing principle in their professional lives. Think of General Lewis Mackenzie, or broadcaster Barbara Frum. Best of all, think of Dr. William Osler. A hundred years ago, Osler revolutionized the practice of medicine not by any startling scientific breakthrough but by insisting that physicians treat the patient, not the disease. He was no goody-goody (he played some wicked practical jokes), but as a clinician, he demonstrated the importance of astute diagnosis, skepticism about unproven treatments, and a humane approach to his patients. He dispelled gloom in the sickroom and inspired hope in his patients. He was an inspirational leader at McGill University in the 1880s, at Johns Hopkins University in Baltimore in the 1890s and early 1900s, and at Oxford University from 1905 until his death in 1919. All three institutions lay claim to his legacy, but he was born in Ontario and his ashes rest in the Osler Library at McGill. And his example lives on in every Canadian health professional who puts healing ahead of profit.
- Creative brilliance. Alice Munro is a hero on two counts. First, she took an underrated literary form—the short story—and produced such polished jewels that she raised standards worldwide. She exemplifies the Canadian ability to colonize a small area of artistry, and enlarge it into an important genre. (We did the same with documentaries and children's music. Another Canadian hero, Wayne Gretzky, performed the same service for hockey.) Second, she has won all the big prizes—the Governor General's, the Giller—yet in typically Canadian style, she refuses to be lionized.

- Humour. How did Canadians ever earn a reputation for being boring when comedians are one of our greatest exports? Perhaps it is because Canadian humour is so dead-pan. When a laugh track is fitted to emigrants like Mike Myers, Martin Short, Jim Carrey, and John Candy, American audiences finally get it. Alongside the irony, in a blazing talent like Rick Mercer, is irreverence and a burning sense of social justice. Mercer illustrates both the Canadian capacity for edgy comedy and our gift for not taking ourselves too seriously. He even gets politicians to laugh at themselves.

- Commitment to the common good. For Canadian peacekeepers, there is no personal glory in what they do. They just put their own lives on the line as they keep warring factions apart. Who doesn't get misty-eyed each time we see those chunky young men in fatigues, with shaven heads and big grins, loading up yet another lumbering Hercules aircraft with medical supplies and basic rations? Whether reassuring Albanians in Kosovo, or helping children in East Timor, they embody the spirit of mutual dependence that kept prairie farmers going during the Great Depression, or propelled Newfoundlanders to help one another when the fishery collapsed.

- Self-invention. The catalogue of our bogus heroes is delightfully long. Laura Secord didn't lead a cow behind the lines in the War of 1812. Grey Owl, the most famous Red Indian in the world, was born Archibald Stansfeld Belaney in Hastings, England. Billy Bishop wasn't quite the fighter pilot ace that the Canadian government claimed. But Canada has given all kinds of people the opportunity to reinvent themselves, and we're really good at it. My particular favourite is Lili St. Cyr, the Montreal stripper who scandalized and seduced Montreal in the 1940s and 1950s. Lili's real name was Marie Van Schaak. She was born in Minneapolis in 1918, and she couldn't speak a word of French. She boasted that she had broken hearts and emptied wallets, but a helluva lot of people had a helluva good time in her presence. And she epitomizes the chameleon quality of Canadians: We adapt to the world around us.

POSTSCRIPT BY
PETER C. NEWMAN

PIERRE ELLIOTT TRUDEAU came the closest to being Canada's modern hero. It was no surprise that just before the millennium, the country's media adjudicators voted him "Top Newsmaker of the Twentieth Century." Certainly, he made news during and long after his sixteen-year reign as Canada's fifteenth prime minister. But that wasn't what made him a hero.

I first became conscious of his heroic qualities in the spring of 1968, at the Liberal Party convention, where enchanted delegates surprised themselves by choosing him as their leader. The cynical political pros—who ran Canada's "governing party," then as now—were accustomed to controlling the succession. Suddenly, they were faced with the prospect of an outsider, who wasn't even a politician, taking the game away from them. I remember watching them, clustered in small worried groups, trying to size up the political magic of this strange and exotic newcomer. Politics is a harsh trade that normally requires half a lifetime's apprenticeship. Yet Trudeau seemed to have mastered its vital elements almost instantly. Only months before, the Montreal law-professor-turned-politician had been proclaiming heretical positions on defence and the social contract, and now here he was, the candidate to beat. They ogled him, chomping their cigars in frustration, scratching their heads, trying to discover if he had some trick they might master.

But they came away puzzled still, telling each other tentatively that it must be his looks or maybe his age, his "radicalism," his money or his reputation as an intellectual. Yet, among his competitors, Robert Winters was handsomer, John Turner younger, Paul Hellyer richer, Eric Kierans more radical, and Paul Martin had as many degrees. But nobody else could draw the crowds, get the laughs, fire the enthusiasm.

They didn't realize that Trudeau had the makings of a hero, and heroism can never be reduced to a formula. It just is. It's a reaction, a feeling, an instant recognition of someone who can enter a room and raise the temperature.

Trudeau had that incandescent glow that thousands of photographers' flash bulbs impart to the flesh, and yet throughout the convention, he appeared remote and austere, his very presence generating an undercurrent of the unexpected. In one of the workshops he was addressing, the solid cadre of photographers and television men who followed his every move was blocking the view of the delegates. Finally, an exasperated delegate stood up and yelled: "Down in front." Trudeau barked back: "How far in front?", quizzically implying that the audience wanted him to sit down. It was a small joke, but it persuaded the photographers to move back, and won him a round of applause.

Any political convention develops into a circus for the candidates, with enough pressure to break the composure of even the strongest psyche. Yet Trudeau maintained a sense of inner repose, and the more he held himself back, the more the crowds wanted a piece of him.

I recall most vividly a middle-aged woman turning to her chubby farmer husband just before Trudeau entered his delegate hospitality suite at the Château Laurier Hotel, and asking him: "What if I faint when he comes in?" The husband, one of those careful Canadians who wore both a belt and suspenders, gave her a look of total disgust. But when Trudeau sauntered by and shook his hand, the farmer's eyes turned moist. He stood there, speech-less, stunned by he-knew-not-what, then hugged his wife.

All through such encounters, Trudeau remained himself, a cool cat in a hot world doing his grainy thing. His style consisted of remaining self-contained, the custodian of his own potential—which, of course is the defining quality of anyone with heroic pretensions.

Heroes involuntarily awaken in others the possibility of real-izing their own aspirations. Coming to power after a decade of the status quo Diefenbaker-Pearson administrations, Trudeau lived up to his campaign slogan: "We need new guys and new ideas!" Few delegates worried about the direction Trudeau was proposing to lead Canada and the Liberal Party; it was enough that they saw in him the "new guy and the new ideas."

Trudeau's unorthodox style held the promise that the process of discovering Canada—and defining ourselves—had not come to an end. This was, after all, the year following Expo 67, and every-thing seemed possible.

Unlike the other candidates, he answered questions not in terms of the past but in terms of an unknown, exciting future. His heroic status grew out of his ability (or was it instinct?) to convey the notion that there was room for honesty and space for intelli-gence in public life. That politics was not just the business of trading power in backrooms but was a way of sharing in the pas-sions of our age.

The delegates at that 1968 leadership convention sensed that they were there at the creation, at the birth, of a genuine Canadian hero. That in Trudeau they had found an unusual meet-ing of a man and his time.

Inevitably, after sixteen years in power, Trudeau lost much of his magic, and most Canadians were as eager to see him go as they had been to welcome him into the nation's highest office. It was easy to argue that in the interval he had lost touch with the masses and retreated into the bureaucratic fortress that is Ottawa. But he was never corrupted by power.

In retrospect, like all heroes, Pierre Trudeau remains a figure of mystery. That was his paradox, and that was what made him heroic: that no matter what he said or what he did, it was never possible to discern what inner forces sustained him. This was the ultimate mystery that made him the source of such fascination— the trick that the professionals at that long-ago leadership convention could never uncover.

QUESTION FIVE

IS THERE
LIFE AFTER
UNITY?

The threat of Quebec separation has dominated Canada's political discourse for the better part of the last half-century. But what if the unity issue could somehow be brought to a successful resolution? What pre-existing or entirely new national preoccupations would claim Canada's political centre stage then?

THE REALITY PRINCIPLE

BY GUY LAFOREST

IF ONE HAD TO WRITE A BOOK on political tragedy in the twentieth century, the pages about Canada would be few and far between. I shall not be sad when I tell my children this. However, it would be wrong to conclude that nothing can be learned from our country's history. One feature of the Canadian experience that can edify our contemporaries is the relationship between federalism and Quebec. I call this "the Great Canadian Paradox."

Since 1945, no province has tried harder than Quebec to reform the institutions of Canadian federalism. Yet insofar as these efforts have often taken the shape of a drive for sovereignty, they have probably also been the biggest obstacle to a successful transformation of the federation. Thus, Quebec simultaneously fuels and chokes the reform engine.

But the paradox can take a different shape.

The Canadian state and Canadian intellectuals are the champions of federalism. Canada is the sponsor of an international organization known as the Forum of Federations, which held its first major conference at Mont-Tremblant, Quebec, in October 1999. Bob Rae, former Ontario premier and major contender for the Liberal leadership in 2006, has played a pivotal role for many years in this association, which has been quite successful in fostering a network of experts and civil servants with differing perspectives on the theory and practice of federalism.

Why is Canada playing a leading role in this network? Michael Ignatieff gave one answer at the beginning of this decade: "Other people besides Canadians should be concerned if Canada dies. If federalism can't work in my Canada, it probably can't work anywhere."

Canadians champion federalism, but since the last Quebec referendum there has been almost no sustained evaluation of the federal political system in this country. Many people believe such an examination would play into the hands of separatists. So what should preoccupy us if the unity issue is ever successfully resolved? I think Canadians should seriously examine the nature and state of their federal institutions, especially the Supreme Court, the Senate, and the powers of the prime minister.

The Supreme Court of Canada, in its 1998 decision on the reference case concerning the secession of Quebec, identified four principles at the heart of our political and legal systems: federalism, democracy, constitutionalism and the rule of law, and respect for the rights of minorities. The judgment was an ode to the nobility and pre-eminence of federalism in Canada. However, I think the Supreme Court neglected the content of our two most important legal documents: the *Constitution* acts of 1867 and 1982.

In 1867, the Canadian Dominion was part of the British Empire. A hierarchical structure was created, with Westminster above the Dominion and the provinces subordinate to Ottawa. British politicians and civil servants were among the Fathers of Confederation, and they made sure the imperial principle would be at least as important as the federal one in the institutional balance of the time. Throughout the twentieth century, Canada gradually liberated itself from Westminster's imperial control over our politics.

However, the same point cannot be made with regard to the relationship between Ottawa and the provinces. Beyond the symbolism of the constitutional monarchy, Ottawa has retained a wide array of powers over the provinces, powers that have more to do with imperialism than with federalism (for instance, the ability to legislate in all fields, to move into the competencies of the provinces and to reserve and disallow provincial legislation). That they are seldom used does not render these powers non-existent. Moreover, their mere existence creates a certain climate, a national political habit of seeing Ottawa as the senior government and the others as distant juniors. Beyond the renewed rhetoric about the number and identity of "nations" within Canada, this imbalance is our real and lasting status quo.

If Canadians are as serious as the Harper government claims to be about the value of federalism, then the legal and political relationships between Ottawa and the provinces should be rebuilt around the idea of balanced coordination. This point has been made eloquently by the champions of federalism in Quebec, from the late André Laurendeau and Claude Ryan to André Burelle and Christian Dufour.

As a guiding star, federalism was not as important in 1867 as the Supreme Court has claimed. Nor was it in 1982. Most experts recognize that the Charter of Rights has weakened the place of the federal principle in our political culture. The first section of the Charter establishes that there are reasonable limits to the exercise of rights in a "free and democratic society." Whenever judges have to interpret this key part of the Charter in constitutional disputes, they are not instructed to take into consideration the federal nature of Canada. If federalism is our guiding star, shouldn't our Charter proclaim to the world that we are a free and democratic federation?

So if the unity issue is ever laid to rest, modernizing institutions to make them compatible with the spirit of federalism should occupy centre stage in Canadian politics. This would involve, first and foremost, a new mechanism for judiciary appointments. Supreme Court justices should not merely be designated by the prime minister. This process has nothing to do with federalism, and it weakens the legitimacy of the tribunal.

The same argument must be made with regard to the Senate. In modern federations, such as Belgium and Germany, second legislative chambers are effective channels of coordination between partners. The Canadian federation has no permanent day-to-day mechanism for this coordination. Ronald Watts, a former principal of Queen's University and Canada's pre-eminent expert on federalism, has this to say about our Senate: "Where senators are appointed by the federal government, as in Canada, they have the least credibility as spokespersons for regional interests, even when they are residents of the regions they represent."

All too often in Canada, reinforcing federalism means strengthening the central government. A reformed Senate would give us a healthier federation by enabling provincial authorities to participate in making legislation at the centre, thereby placing additional checks and balances in the working of our institutions.

Championing federalism in Canada will also require curtailing the privileges of the prime minister, currently invested with the powers of an emperor, as we have been reminded by Donald Savoie, past president of the Canadian Political Science Association and one of our leading scholars on governance: "Concentrating so much power in the hands of one individual and a handful of courtiers is fraught with danger." Savoie's remarks were addressed to the regime of Jean Chrétien, but they remain as valid in the Harper era. The Report of the Gomery Commission has reinforced this point by insisting on the need for greater legislative control of the executive branch of government.

Changing the way Supreme Court judges are nominated and redesigning the Senate would significantly reduce the powers of the prime minister. What else could be done? I think our current practice of ad hoc federal-provincial conferences should be replaced by a federal council co-chaired by the prime minister and a representative from the group of premiers. The current process, which allows Ottawa to dictate the agenda and control the meetings, reflects much that is wrong with federalism in Canada.

No matter what happens to the Canadian federation in the years to come, I will, of course, teach my kids that Canada deserves its reputation as an extraordinary country. However, I will add that our political system does not measure up to our fame abroad. We talk more about federalism than we practise in our institutions. If we can ever get beyond the impasse with Quebec, we should act more and talk less.

A country such as Canada has a great deal to teach the world, and Quebec could make a huge contribution.

BETRAYING A HIGHER VISION

BY OVIDE MERCREDI

UNFORTUNATELY, MANY CANADIANS assume unity is a problem only for the predominantly anglophone state and its francophone minorities. But aboriginal people see the future of the country and the issue of national unity in a different way. Canadian unity does not belong exclusively to the white colonizers, any more than it is the fate of aboriginal people to accept their displacement from their ancestral homeland. And so I see two potential scenarios for the day after the unity debate ends, one of an exclusionary Canada, the other of an inclusionary Canada. I will deal with the former in this essay and the latter in my postscript.

An exclusionary Canada presumes that Quebec and the rest of Canada have reached a new understanding that brings unity for anglophones and francophones, but that once again excludes indigenous peoples from the unity talks. Too cynical? Perhaps. But such marginalization of aboriginal peoples is well documented by history and by our contemporary experience within Canada. One need only remember the vision of Confederation chosen in 1867 and, more recently, during the failed Meech Lake Accord.

I now begin my journey into the crystal ball of exclusionary Canada—"the day after."

It is hard for me to imagine how this has happened again. How can national unity be achieved without the participation of the aboriginal people who possess a pre-existing title to the very soil that Canada now claims as its territory? Aboriginal peoples have long feared that any mission to rebuild Canada without them can only be achieved at the expense of their rights, including their sovereignty over their lands and territories. Their fears were well founded.

Canada's justification for excluding aboriginal people this time was the same excuse used in the Meech Lake Accord negotiations. They told us our concerns would complicate matters, would distract from the issue paramount to the country's survival: Quebec's status within Canada. They assured us our place in Canada would be dealt with later, after national unity was achieved between Quebec and the rest of the federation. And so, only two groups of people were deemed to be the natural architects of Canada's survival: the English and the French.

This great achievement (at least in the minds of the colonizers) is received across the country with jubilant celebrations, except in aboriginal communities. Now that the two titans have finished fighting over the scraps of power and jurisdiction— their idea of building unity—what is left to share with the aboriginal peoples?

Governments failed once again to understand that recognizing aboriginal peoples as equals in the process of reforming Canada is the road to justice and reconciliation. There is no other. Without the participation of aboriginal peoples, no one will ever find the elusive medicine needed to cure disharmony, separation, and regional conflict. To find peace between Quebec and the rest of the country without securing unity with aboriginal peoples would be to do as the white Fathers of Confederation did in Charlottetown: to build a country for two races, ignoring the original peoples as if they were irrelevant, a hindrance to their dream.

Do the white politicians not realize that the future belongs to everybody, not just a select few? Aboriginal peoples have a human right to shape their own destiny as distinct peoples; the continued exclusion of aboriginal peoples diminishes the great potential and glory of this country as a haven for people from different cultures.

The argument that our place in the future of this country can be dealt with after national unity is achieved ignores our history. We have lived on this land for centuries. Do the English and the French have a greater claim? If so, on what is it based? The principle of occupation, or of racial superiority? Our roots in this land precede by centuries those of Quebec and the rest of Canada. Today, aboriginal title is law in Canada. How can anyone hope to hide from that truth?

We can all agree that the participation of aboriginal peoples in the restructuring of Canada might bring more challenges in the quest for unity. But to exclude aboriginal peoples because too many challenges increase the likelihood of failure is dishonest and cowardly. To favour political expediency rather than to face reality mocks Canada's deeply cherished principles of democracy and fairness for all.

The reaffirmation of the status quo—"two founding nations"—is a betrayal of the higher vision that calls for the establishment of a new country inclusive of all people, including aboriginal people. In reinforcing the myth of the "two founding nations," Canada chooses to remain a nation-state anchored in an outdated national identity. For the majority of Canadians who voted yes in a referendum on keeping Quebec within the federation, the exclusion of indigenous peoples was a small price to pay to preserve national unity. Very Canadian, eh?

But somewhere in Canada an indigenous elder shakes her head in disbelief. She speaks gently to her grandchildren: "My grandchildren, the white people are not ready to accept us. We have to wait. The road ahead will not be easy. It was hard for us. It may be even harder for you. But we must not give up hope. In time the white governments will have to honour their promises made to our people a long time ago. The Creator is kind; someday we will walk a lot easier on our road. Be patient, my grandchildren, you will see this come to pass."

Somewhere else in Canada a loud noise is heard as a hydro line comes crashing down on the new "O Canada." In the halls of aboriginal assemblies across the land, a debate is raging on the great betrayal. Many leaders of the first peoples advocate non-violent civil disobedience. Many aboriginal people agree, for the first time, that separation and sovereignty for the first peoples is the only real option available.

Somewhere in the halls of power of the new Canada, the police are put on notice to maintain peace and order for the new country; white politicians in every part of Canada urge aboriginal people to respect the rule of law.

The first peoples' strongest leaders and elders are on their way to the United Nations to appeal for their human rights, including their right to self-determination. Indigenous peoples from all over the world join in the call to establish a mechanism under the United Nations for the decolonization of indigenous peoples and lands. Indigenous elders and visionaries welcome this movement as a fulfillment of ancient prophecies predicting the establishment of a New World of peace and harmony for all peoples, not just a world controlled by nation-states.

In the meantime, the new Canada smugly celebrates its cherished unity. It's back to business as usual in the rest of the new Canada.

POSTSCRIPT BY
GUY LAFOREST

CANADA AND QUEBEC HAVE major responsibilities with regard to the fate of their native peoples. The issues concerning indigenous peoples, such as identity, self-government, and recognition, have become urgent in many countries of the Americas. Mexico, Guatemala, Ecuador, and Peru have frequently made headlines on this matter in the past few years. In these lands, rising expectations have been voiced with a combination of despair, angry rhetoric, and violence. None of these countries operates politically in the context of a stabilized liberal democracy, as Canada does. This background illustrates both our challenge and our additional burden as the United Nations system of organizations sails through a Decade of Partnership with the Indigenous Peoples of the Earth (1994–2004).

Throughout the 1990s, I enjoyed many opportunities to see at work the wisdom, persuasive rhetoric, and leadership qualities of Ovide Mercredi. I have often said to myself that he would be a better prime minister for Canada than many of those that we have had, including the present one. There is great nobility in his vision of seeking justice and a lasting constitutional peace on the basis of the consent and participation of the native peoples, rather than having a constitutional order imposed on them once more. Still, serious disagreements remain between us. Some of the most important of these are related to the interpretation of key periods of our constitutional dialogue: 1867 and the *British North America Act*, the constitutional revision of 1982 and the Meech Lake saga (1987–1990).

Mr. Mercredi reads the founding debates, which took place between 1864 and 1867, and which led to the emergence of a federation of British colonies enjoying Dominion status in the Empire, in agreement with the dominant vision in French-Canadian historiography. In Quebec and French Canada, Confederation has, indeed, often been interpreted as a pact between two nations, or two founding peoples. Some French Canadians, such as Cartier, Taché, and Langevin, were included in the talks that occurred at the time, while native peoples and their leaders were not. In addition, there were a number of dualistic elements concerning the French- and English-speaking peoples, the Catholics and the Protestants, Quebec, and the other colonial territories in the legal documents that came out of Westminster.

Confederation was not, however, first and foremost a pact between two peoples. Rather, in the famous words of the late Arthur Lower, one of the leading Canadian historians of the twentieth century, the British colonies in North America were placed in the crucible of imperial omnicompetence, and they came out remelted, shining, new, and fused. The native peoples, like all the others, were thrown into that crucible, landing squarely with their narrowly circumscribed territories, in Section 91(24) of the *British North America Act*, thus falling under the trusteeship of the federal government. All in all, it is fair to say that colonial leaders, in the United Canadas, in Nova Scotia, and in New Brunswick, ultimately consented to this rearrangement. Nobody cared whether the native peoples would have given their consent if the powers in place had seen fit to ask them. In truth, nobody asked for the consent of the French- and English-speaking peoples either. Popular ratification was simply not part of our political culture at the time.

Mr. Mercredi argues that the native peoples were marginalized in 1867, and excluded once again in the debates surrounding the Meech Lake Accord. Oddly enough, he fails to mention the reforms of 1981–82. Yet Canada's First Nations were certainly not consulted by Prime Minister Pierre Trudeau prior to his patriation endeavours. Moreover, native leaders opposed his projects vigorously in Canada and abroad, mounting a strong, albeit unsuccessful, challenge in London. Compared with what Mr. Trudeau had in mind fifteen years earlier, when he was minister of justice, the 1982 package was significantly less ambitious. It is regrettable that so few Canadians remember this chapter of our history. In 1967–68, Mr. Trudeau sought a modernization of the political system that would have achieved the following objectives: bringing the constitution back to Canada with a new Charter of Rights; federalizing central institutions such as the Senate and the Supreme Court; rebalancing the division of powers; and, finally, eliminating quasi-imperial devices such as the declaratory power and the dispositions concerning the reservation and disallowance of provincial legislation.

I strongly believe that the way the reform was carried through in the early 1980s and the changes that were achieved—most notably the inclusion of a Charter of Rights aimed at solidifying the unconditional allegiance of scores of Canadians to the central national government—are big obstacles against progress on the other items of Mr. Trudeau's 1967–68 agenda. In sum, the revision of 1982 halted the process that would have led to a more thorough federalization of the Canadian political system.

It is easy to understand why Mr. Mercredi is less troubled by the marginalization of the First Nations in 1982. They secured through this reform an important foothold in the legal tables of the land. In sections 25 and 35 of the 1982 *Constitution Act*, the existence of their ancestral rights was confirmed, and a process was defined to further specify and enshrine their right to self-government. They were left out of the negotiating room; they remained steadfastly opposed to the reform and never gave their consent to it. But recent history and jurisprudence have demonstrated that these legal foundations have allowed them to make significant progress.

If we forget, for a brief moment, the Meech Lake Accord, we find that the momentum created by the presence of sections 25 and 35 in the patriation package led to a comprehensive program for native self-government in the 1992 Charlottetown Agreement. That agreement was finally voted down across Canada, and, in Quebec, in a referendum. It was clearly rejected by the native peoples themselves. Tabling its report in late 1996, the Royal Commission on the Aboriginal Peoples of Canada elaborated in great detail yet another comprehensive blueprint for self-government. So far, this vision has found better allies on the benches of the Supreme Court of Canada than in the cabinet room of the Chrétien government. This global systematic approach was never ratified in an election or a referendum by the peoples of Canada and Quebec, or by the First Nations themselves. The peoples have been marginalized.

The heart of my disagreement with Ovide Mercredi concerns the Meech Lake Accord. On this issue, I think his reasoning is flawed. Like many opponents of the Accord, he has often argued as if it would have cleanly replaced the 1982 package, whereas it was essentially meant to complement it. Granted, it spoke a lot more about Quebec than it did about native peoples. However, it would not, in any way whatsoever, have affected the legal weight and meaning of sections 25 and 35 of the 1982 constitution. And Meech Lake included a lot about Quebec because 1982 did not. To use Mr. Mercredi's words, it was Quebec that was marginalized in 1982. The most important transformations of our legal and political landscape in the twentieth century were made over and against the objections of Quebec. Fairness has its requirements. If the people of Quebec were not asked to ratify, neither were the people of Canada. In the same spirit of fairness, I would make the following concession to Ovide Mercredi. It was reasonable for native leaders to believe a decade ago that any momentum for constitutional change, for their own much desired constitutional changes, would have been reduced after the passage of the Meech Lake Accord.

Where does this leave us? I think it leaves us with a complex history, with many narratives of exclusion and a number of missed opportunities. Canada is home to more than two founding peoples. Too many groups have ended, at times, on the marginalized side of things. At the same time, it leaves all of us, in comparative perspective, with an interesting starting place for the twenty-first century. I am reasonably optimistic for Quebec and for Canada. I know we have much to learn from the native peoples of this country. And I look forward to many stimulating encounters with Ovide Mercredi.

POSTSCRIPT BY
OVIDE MERCREDI

UNITY IS EXACTING, not easily obtained through myths of patriotism or pride in a beautiful country. As the framers of a newly constituted Canada—a Canada that has at last resolved the unity question—would find out, national unity, per se, must take a back seat to the needs of the people.

A country is more than the sum total of its governmental institutions—local, provincial or national. It is certainly more than a fictional or imposed "national identity" and a flag. It is far more than its art, music, or picture shows. A country is about its people and their needs, the preservation of the natural environment and all forms of life and the survival of a peaceful and civil society. In short, if a country is inclusive, it is about the quality of life for all, not just for the wealthy or the fortunate. If Canada is to become embraced by aboriginal people, the past relationship, based on the denial of indigenous rights and on the exclusion of aboriginal people from the progress or advancement of this country, cannot carry into this new millennium.

Today, the needs of aboriginal peoples are many. This was not always so. Years of isolation, exclusion and neglect of our rights have resulted in our displacement from our lands, the breakdown of our economy, the loss of our culture, the denial of our power to govern ourselves, and the deplorable poverty that is now an integral part of our identity within Canada. Aboriginal peoples deserve much more than the status of supplicants and dependants that this country has imposed on them in the past century. Their endless fight to find justice in their homeland is a black mark on this country that portrays itself so proudly in the international community as the model of human rights and freedoms. At some point in aboriginal and Canadian relations, aboriginal people should begin to enjoy the freedom of living in a free and democratic society that embraces their unique and distinct status as first peoples and values their collective rights as indigenous peoples. In other words, generations after generations of aboriginal peoples should not have to fight for their basic human rights to their lands and resources, languages and cultures, and to earn a livelihood.

To ignore the needs of aboriginal peoples, as Canada's political and economic elite have often attempted to do, or to dismiss them as irrelevant to the higher goal of building a strong united country, is to jeopardize the future of Canada. Aboriginal peoples are no less important than Quebec to the maintenance of unity in this country. Aboriginal people know that Canada was a compromise experiment in nation-building between English and French factions who felt the threats of the expansionism of the United States. We also hold the view that neither the English nor the French had any business creating a country on our lands without our consent. For that reason, and the injustices that this union spawned, aboriginal nations do not get too excited by the prospect that Canada is about to implode. Of course, we care about the outcome of the current struggle between Quebec and the rest of Canada. We care, as our ancestors did at the time of Confederation, for our land and our future. That commitment to our survival as First Peoples on our side of Mother Earth explains our determination not to allow Canada (including Quebec) to set the stage and rules in this millennium.

Quebec has long argued that outmoded concepts of confederation and federalism can no longer sustain unity. Something more than the status quo is needed to keep the coexistence of different founding peoples a reality in this country. On this point, aboriginal peoples are in agreement with Quebec that fundamental reforms are needed to maintain the coexistence of different peoples, something so different and substantial that it will capture the loyalty of all the people. In other words, we need to build a better and more inclusive country—a statement that implies Canada can be perfected.

To that end, building a country based on the principle of inclusiveness would be preferable to maintaining a nation-state that primarily serves the needs of urban dwellers and non-aboriginal Canadians. In seeking to strengthen Canada, the hopes and aspirations of aboriginal peoples, visible minorities, women, the West, and Quebec cannot be ignored. Canada must come to understand that it is more than its cities and capitals. It is far more than fiscal or monetary policy. It is more than the Parliament that now governs in a false pretense of democracy. It is more than all its institutions combined. In fact, Canada is an idea that is still very much incomplete.

The greatest ambitions of aboriginal peoples are to restore and reclaim their assaulted cultures and languages, to own land and resources, to rebuild their economy and to re-establish governments based on indigenous concepts of consensual democracy that will provide their people with the legacy of good government Canada has failed to provide. Contrary to the negative voices, such as those of the Reform Party, the restoration of the aboriginal peoples' capacity to look after themselves is the medicine we need to cure the ills that plague Canadian and aboriginal relations. Assimilation and the disappearance of collective aboriginal identities in favour of a "Canadian identity" are not the answer.

Our vision as aboriginal peoples does not revolve exclusively around the goal of reclaiming our indigenous collective rights, heritage, and future. In tandem with the preservation of our indigenous societies, we are equally engaged in a quest to come to terms with how we can belong to and participate in the national life of Canada without the fear of full assimilation. Our vision includes respect for civil and human rights and the freedom of individuals to participate in the national life of Canada, free from discrimination, racism, or poverty. Without question, we want to be treated with respect and dignity by the rest of Canada. Unfortunately, for generations of aboriginal peoples, the dream of individual equality remains as elusive as our belief that someday this country will realize that its greatness lies in the recognition and advancement of the distinct rights and freedoms of aboriginal nations.

These two goals of remaining distinct peoples and belonging as equals to a larger national community, such as a country, are not irreconcilable dreams. They are based on a hopeful vision that would allow our people to be themselves, to advance as distinct peoples and yet to remain contributing citizens of a country that has ceased to hurt them.

Can we move on and get on with our lives? Can we do it alone? Perhaps we will all discover in time that we all need each other. So let us assume that one day Canada achieves its cherished unity. Let's assume that federalism has been modified to accommodate the needs of aboriginal peoples, Quebec, visible minorities, women, and the West. Let's also assume that the vast majority of the population is in support of the new road and a new approach to building a united country.

All these gains mean very little unless accompanied by concerted and sustained action by governments and the people. It is the day after national unity: what needs to be done?

The new Canada acknowledges that the human condition of aboriginal peoples must be a priority for all governments. A new national program to be led by aboriginal governments is established to bring aboriginal people and communities to the same standard and quality of life that the majority of Canadians have been enjoying for decades. This new program, called the "Four Directions Strategy for Social Equality," aims at immediate and long-term improvements to quality-of-life issues by introducing new measures for housing, education, health, and jobs for all aboriginal people regardless of residence. An important feature of this national action is a joint policy that binds all provinces to the principle and goal of uplifting the economic standing and capacity of aboriginal peoples by providing immediate access to natural resources within their traditional territories for their management and development.

Another important component of this new priority for the united Canada is to build opportunities for aboriginal youth in the national economic life. Aboriginal governments, now having the lead role in rebuilding their economies, have targeted special initiatives for those aboriginal youth who have, for whatever reason, dropped out of the educational system and society. The goal here is to ensure that opportunities for jobs and education are established by aboriginal governments that will lead to greater job opportunities for aboriginal youth in both the traditional and modern economy. Jobs, and not welfare, are seen by all as the greatest equalizer to the lack of social and economic opportunities.

For the first time in Canadian history, the Constitution guarantees that concrete action must be made to uphold the rights of the First Nations, the Inuit, and the Métis. After years of constitutional squabbling, all parties come to accept that only constitutional guarantees to self-government, land, and resources can end the marginalization of indigenous peoples.

As a result of the constitutional reforms, the aboriginal peoples are now free from the indignity of having to prove to Canada that they have aboriginal and treaty rights to land, resources and self-determination. Aboriginal people are now beginning to redirect their energies towards rebuilding their cultures, languages and economies, instead of wasting scarce human and fiscal resources fighting against the powerful resistance by federal and provincial governments to the implementation of their indigenous rights and freedoms.

Another priority task of the new Canada is to care for all its people. A national plan to end poverty, involving all governments (including the now constitutionally recognized governments of aboriginal peoples), must be developed. In a civil and democratic country, the quality of life of its citizens cannot be left to the gambles of a free enterprise system that generates wealth for some, but not for all. A Canada that has affirmed more inclusive, egalitarian values, such as the fair distribution of wealth to the people, must do business in a different fashion than the practice of the past century, which has concentrated the acquisition and distribution of wealth in a few regions.

In developing this new approach to equity in the distribution of wealth, Canada's poor are given a voice in shaping a way out of their poverty. Sharing the wealth of this new country through more equitable distribution of fiscal resources to all governments, and generating new wealth by way of an economic development policy that reaches out to all regions of the country, will prove to be a major task. Without strong government support for free education and health care, opportunities for individuals to improve their standard of living will be ad hoc and meagre, as in the past. (Did I neglect to mention the new Constitution states that education and health are two of the most fundamental human rights of all citizens of the new Canada?)

A third important task for the new Canada is to take a national inventory of the ways and means by which past parliaments, legislatures, and governments, working in collusion with industry, have spoiled the natural environment. A national plan involving all governments and stakeholders has been identified as necessary to the survival of Canada. A national policy to save the environment is deemed as essential by all governments to help regenerate and restore the natural environment for future generations. It seems that the aim for national unity was tempered by the realization that the country couldn't survive, regardless of political will, if the earth is destroyed by the insatiable demand for economic development and the acquisition of wealth. By the way, this new commitment to the environment is not anti-development, but it nonetheless provides a greater commitment to clean air, water, and the earth than is embodied by the idea of "sustainable development." According to my crystal ball, the new Canadian Constitution provides for the constitutional protection of the natural environment for the benefit of future generations. It turns out that environmental preservation and restoration are some of the aboriginal management ideas the new Canada decided to adopt to guarantee its own survival.

Our new Constitution also says racial and cultural tolerance is a fundamental constitutional principle. All governments undertake to develop plans and actions for the building of a new society with zero tolerance for racism, prejudice, and discrimination of any kind. In a world full of ethnic and racial tensions resulting in violence and wars, a new Canada embarking in this direction is expected to demonstrate much-needed leadership in racial and ethnic harmony.

The new Canada also needs new institutions of government that increase citizen participation and supplement a system of representation that now protects only existing power elites and the provinces with the largest populations. One modification made to Parliament, designed to give an appropriate and important role to aboriginal nations, is the constitutional guarantee of seats in the House of Commons for elected representatives of the aboriginal peoples. But the more important departure from the old democracy of representation by population is the introduction of a new national institution with the power to review and amend laws of Parliament and legislatures that derogate from aboriginal and treaty rights—the First Peoples Parliament. This new co-governing body was established at the national level to implement the reforms and changes needed to accommodate aboriginal nations, with the authority to appoint the minister responsible for aboriginal relations and an aboriginal member to the Supreme Court of Canada.

Other perfections to Canada, such as a more equitable sharing of powers, have been agreed to, making it possible for aboriginal governments to cooperate, for example, in the development and preservation of natural resources. Revenue sharing between all governments is now a constitutional imperative. A permanent independent commission comprised of representatives of the different governments is to be established in the future with a mandate to monitor and hold all governments accountable to the new constitutional requirement for the equitable sharing of revenue for the equal benefit of all the people.

The day after this new vision for a more democratic Canada under a new constitutional order is accepted by all the people, the hard work of building a true civilization begins.

Is national unity too exacting for you?

WHEN CANADA SPEAKS, DOES THE WORLD LISTEN?

During the Cold War, Canada enjoyed considerable influence as a middle power. What are the defining characteristics of the post–Cold War world and how do they affect Canadian interests abroad? What steps can Canada take to ensure a prominent voice in world affairs in this new century?

A RECIPE FOR WORLD INFLUENCE

BY ALLAN GOTLIEB

THE HISTORY OF CANADIAN FOREIGN policy is relatively simple: before the First World War it was determined in London; in the interwar years it was isolationist, except when we were supporting the British (which we did even when this conflicted with our national interest); and during the Second World War and the Cold War it was directed at our maintenance of international peace and security, as a NATO member and as a leading middle power in the UN seeking to broker solutions.

What should Canada's foreign policy be in the years ahead? This will depend on our interests and values. But it will also depend on a great unknown: the kind of international order that will prevail in the twenty-first century.

How can one define the post–Cold War environment? Not even two decades old, this reality has defied the prophets by failing to produce a more harmonious "new international order." It has produced, instead, an international landscape unprecedented in modern history. The post–Cold War system is characterized by the most asymmetrical distribution of power since, perhaps, the Roman Empire. The U.S. alone occupies commanding heights in all fields of advanced technology. The U.S. stock market represents more than half the total capitalization of the global market. Meanwhile, the economic decline of Russia continues unabated,

European economic growth is stalled and much of Asia is in economic turmoil. U.S. military power won the war in Kosovo, and all of America's allies (and enemies) know it. U.S. military power pulls farther and farther ahead of its friends', many of whose leaders talk wistfully about the importance of their "soft power." Thanks to U.S. hegemony, NATO has transformed itself from a defensive alliance into the primary peacekeeping force in the world, while the United Nations becomes increasingly marginalized.

But the asymmetrical concentration of power is not the only unusual feature of the post–Cold War era. There are others:

- The emergence of a new zeitgeist. Human rights and humanitarianism have become dominant public concerns, and consequently there is a growing tendency to reject national sovereignty as a legal wall behind which atrocities can be committed.
- Civil wars and the disintegration of states. Internal conflicts, not interstate aggression, are now a paramount threat to international peace. So, too, is the proliferation of states possessing nuclear weapons and of rogue states with access to weapons of mass destruction.
- The growth of a judicialized approach to state behaviour. Some examples of this phenomenon are the rise of judicial procedures in the new World Trade Organization, the establishment of an International Criminal Court and the proliferation of ad hoc tribunals to prosecute crimes against humanity.

Canadian foreign policy has veered away from traditional international security concerns and towards the objectives of trade enhancement and the promotion of "human security," with little to connect the two. No real purpose is served by trying to embrace them in some overarching general strategy, such as the pursuit of a human security agenda; some of our objectives are selfish, some not.

If, in this new century, Canadian interests and the international environment do not shift dramatically, we can probably identify a mix of objectives—some economic, some political, some humanitarian—as the basis of our foreign policy. Among them are likely to be the global pursuit of Canadian economic advantage; the achievement of more secure access to U.S. markets; and the ability to contribute to peacekeeping initiatives, the protection of human rights, and the alleviation of poverty.

Whether Canada achieves these goals will depend largely on one factor: the influence we are able to bring to bear beyond our borders. This, in turn, will depend on whether we learn to appreciate the assets we have at our disposal and on how well we use them.

Foremost among these assets is our privileged relationship with the United States. Our ability to influence U.S. foreign policy far surpasses in importance any other manner in which we might seek to affect the course of international events. The Canadian voice is listened to with respect in the U.S. corridors of power; it is likened to the voice of a family member. Canadians make an unpardonable error if they fail to realize this.

Another key asset, often underrated by Canadians, is Canada's historical and cultural affinity with Europe. Over the years, most Canadian political leaders have been uncomfortable in dealing with the Europeans, including even the British. They have seriously underestimated the significance of the emergence of the European superpower. Few international initiatives will go far without its support. A prime example of our tendency to waste this asset was our provocative behaviour in the fisheries dispute with Spain, which damaged our relationship with the European Union for an extended period.

A third asset is a Canadian population that is internationalist in outlook and sympathetic to humanitarian considerations. This places Canada in a strong position to contribute to the major global challenge of the new millennium: defining the scope of humanitarian interventions and making them more effective. But to capitalize on this position, Canada needs to follow a consistent approach to recognizing human rights. The Canadian government has not always done this. (Although it deserves credit for efforts to distance itself from the oppressive Castro regime in Cuba.)

Equally important, the Canadian public must begin to understand that without the necessary investment in "hard power," i.e., military capability, our efforts to play a significant role in humanitarian interventions are likely to be regarded more as posturing than as a serious national commitment.

There is no element more critical to influence in foreign policy than the human resources employed to design and conduct it. Knowledge of foreign languages, cultures, and history; analytical skills; excellent judgment refined through sustained experience—these are the essential ingredients of a recipe that will produce influential diplomats and foreign-policy advisers. Alas, the recipe is rarely followed these days. We can speak with a loud voice in the world, but if we have nothing intelligent or constructive to say, who will listen?

Finally, there is the strength of our legal tradition. As distinctions break down between national sovereignty and domestic jurisdiction, as concern over international criminal behaviour grows, as international economic behaviour becomes increasingly constrained by quasi-judicial review, one of the foremost instruments of influence will be a nation's jurists, legally trained diplomats, and judicial tradition.

Throughout most of the twentieth century, international law was marginalized; this is now rapidly changing. It is noteworthy that Canada's record before the World Trade Organization in recent times has not been good. Once again, if we wish to see our values and interests promoted on the international stage, Canadians must be ready to invest in developing an outstanding cadre of experts in the field of international law.

Of course, nurturing such assets and using them well is not glamorous, nor is it the stuff of headlines. But it is the stuff of influence, without which Canadians will not make a difference in the world.

DEVELOPING A NATIONAL VOICE

BY JANICE GROSS STEIN

IN A GLOBAL ECONOMY, SOVEREIGNTY is no longer what it was and states no longer have the same power to protect, or to abuse, their citizens. Canada is no exception: it is but a shadow of its former self, with only a whisper for a voice. On this, Canadian champions and the critics of "globalization" agree.

But both are wrong. Each underestimates the capacity Canada retains to make a difference on global issues, even as the face of sovereignty changes.

We can only make a difference, however, if we build the domestic platform needed to participate effectively in a knowledge-based global system; what we do at home shapes our choices abroad.

In the post–Cold War world, powerful enemies are largely absent and global market forces are ever-present. In the global marketplace, Canada is not as significant a player as it was fifty years ago, and it is likely to become even less important as China, India, Brazil, Argentina, and Indonesia mature. Canada also faces a special challenge: it lives next door to the mighty United States.

The most serious threat to Canada's survival as a nation with a distinct identity is no longer military attack, but the pull and push of the U.S. economy and its entertainment industries. More and more innovative, risk-acceptant young Canadians are being drawn to the United States to work. More and more Canadians are watching programs produced in the United States, listening to music by American recording artists, and reading books and magazines written and edited in the United States.

It is no surprise that managing the Canada-U.S. relationship is front and centre on our government's agenda. If there is to be a Canada at all—much less a Canada that speaks with authority on global issues—strategic choices must be made.

Ottawa, the provincial governments and the private sector must invest strategically in educating a scientifically and technically literate population and in promoting innovation. We have had a decade of investment in our research and scientific infrastructure, but much more remains to be done. We still lag badly behind other G8 countries in our investments in science, research, and commercialization.

Telecommunications and computer companies, software developers and biotechnology firms must partner with universities, colleges and governments to provide world-class opportunities for young Canadians. How Canada will fare in a global knowledge-based economy will depend largely on the skills of our citizens. Here we must do far better than in the past if Canada is to be a player in global markets.

But scientific and technical literacy alone will not provide a sufficient platform for authoritative participation in world politics. Canadians know alarmingly little about their own history, and they are unfamiliar with the cultures and practices of their diverse fellow citizens. Our schools, post-secondary institutions and national public broadcaster must do significantly better in teaching Canadians about the richness of their past and the diversity of their present.

Participation in global politics is no longer restricted to a cadre of trained experts, as it was half a century ago. In the future, larger and larger numbers of Canadians will move abroad, come home and move out again. If we do not know our history, we will quickly forget who we are as we spend more time away from home. Canadian identity will blur and Canada's voice will gradually become mute.

We will also be unable to exploit one of our most important assets in global politics—our richly diverse population. Networks of immigrants now connect Canada around the globe. These networks are invaluable channels as Canada seeks to make its voice heard on international issues. We should lead in developing practices of multiple citizenship to strengthen these connections. Access to Canadian citizenship should be made easier rather than more difficult. Much of our recent discussion about dual citizenship misses the enormous advantages that these citizens bring, through the bridges they build and cross. Canadians who move in and out of the country strengthen our international connections and help "brand" Canada to those who might not know us otherwise.

But even if we invest strategically in engineering a better knowledge platform than we have in the past, living permanently in the shadow of the United States is still no easy task. It is even harder now, in this "unipolar" moment.

Canada must watch its economic back continuously. It does, and should, devote a great deal of attention to monitoring and lobbying Washington. Officials must also use the dense networks of political, social, and economic connections between Canadians and Americans to promote Canadian interests in Washington. We must also continue to promote multilateral regimes and rules of fair play. Logic dictates that Canada will generally do better on a regulated multilateral playing field than in one-to-one contests with Washington. When there is no choice but to deal with an issue bilaterally, there will inevitably be conflict and compromise; Canada will win some, but lose more.

Above all, Canada must have a responsible, independent voice in global politics. What Canada says and does globally helps us to define ourselves, and we have the power to speak strategically in several important ways. We can, for example, lead where the United States—particularly the executive branch—wishes it could go but sometimes cannot. We did so recently, for example, in Haiti, and at the United Nations when we led the General Assembly to engineer the passage of the "Responsibility to Protect," and charted the path for management reform, a very important but neglected and difficult issue for the UN. Despite the occasional rhetoric to the contrary in Congress, Canada's leadership was helpful, and was seen as helpful, to the American government.

Canada can also speak directly to some of the most difficult problems bedevilling the global system. Ethnic and religious intolerance, governments unaccountable to their citizens, legal systems ungoverned by the rule of law, social inequity, and the fracturing of communities in an age of global markets—all often spill over into violence. Canadian culture in its deepest sense—our habits of diversity, our respect for human rights and our civility— provides the kind of expertise needed when the big powers or international institutions seek to prevent conflict or to reconstruct war-torn societies.

A decade ago, Canada took the lead on a basket of humanitarian issues—the ban on land mines, the creation of an International Criminal Court—and built a coalition of twelve states, including Norway and South Africa, committed to enhancing the protection of citizens, even, if necessary, against their own governments. Seizing the moment when sovereignty is in retreat, Canada made a difference globally. We can continue to do so if we use our human resources well and choose our issues carefully. But this capacity for significant engagement in global politics will be impaired if we are reduced to echoing the United States. Unease with the weight of American economic, cultural, military, and political power is not just a Canadian concern: Europe and Japan are worried as well, and they are not stilling their voices. On the right issues, it is imperative that Canada have an independent voice, even if that voice occasionally irritates our neighbours.

The gravest threat, not only to our capacity to engage in the world but also to our survival, is our tendency to whisper or echo when we can indeed speak and make a difference.

POSTSCRIPT BY
ALLAN GOTLIEB

"THE MOST SERIOUS THREAT to Canada's survival is no longer military attack, but the pull and push of the U.S. economy and its entertainment industries." Thus writes Janice Gross Stein. If this is Canada's greatest threat, we are indeed a blessed nation. But is it true?

Canada has enjoyed a century and a half of peace with the United States. And thanks to the prosperity that has come with good relations, over a third of our total wealth is derived from U.S. markets. Hollywood has been in business most of this century, but we are still around. Can you imagine the outrage in Toronto and Vancouver if, as some Americans propose, the U.S. were to ban off-shore production of Hollywood films? If the entertainment industry is our most serious threat, why did Ottawa license giant ears on our southern boundary to capture popular programs from the U.S. television networks and carry them by cable into virtually every Canadian household? We know why. Canadians wanted them. The truth is there are probably no two nations in the world that, thanks to shared values and cultural affinities, have enjoyed a more enduring friendship. This probably explains why Canadians tend to think of foreign policy as relating to everything in the world—the UN, the Third World, the Commonwealth—except the United States. Many of us take our relations with the U.S. for granted. We believe that the U.S. has an obligation to be nice to us whether or not we are nice to them. But if our political survival does not depend on relations with the U.S., our prosperity does.

That is why the greatest foreign-policy challenge for Canada is the management of our relations with the U.S.

Because of the enormous disparity between our size, wealth, and power, there is a profound asymmetry in our respective foreign policies; the Americans' biggest foreign-policy challenge is assuredly not the management of its relationship with Canada. This places Canada in a particularly vulnerable position. Our vulnerability is further enhanced by two other asymmetries.

While there is a high degree of economic integration between our two countries, there is absolutely no political integration. Consequently, unlike in the case of the European Community, there are no common political bodies that can guarantee Canadian participation in U.S. decision-making and thus help ensure fairness.

The third asymmetry compounds the effect of the other two. At the Canadian national level, political power is concentrated in the federal cabinet, while in the U.S. it is far more dispersed, even atomized. U.S. senators and congressmen exercise power analogous to the executive in a parliamentary system; they routinely initiate legislation and administrative actions in response to protectionist-minded special interests. The devastating history of measures taken against our softwood lumber industry is particularly illustrative. Yet one must not lose sight of the fact that the president wields far greater influence with Congress than any foreign power could ever aspire to. While threats to our economic and other interests can arise from within the executive branch (e.g., split-runs and new restrictions on defence contracting), most disputes, from softwood to Helms-Burton, seem to originate in the Congress and associated regulatory bodies. Such threats are not only deeply damaging, they are almost never definitively resolved. For this reason, Canada cannot be merely responsive;

notwithstanding the risks, it must make itself part of the American internal process.

Thus, the supreme Canadian challenge is to manage relations not just with "the government of the United States," but with a highly fragmented system of governance in the most powerful nation in the world. What does this mean for the actual conduct of our relations with the United States?

First and foremost, the relationship must be the constant pre-occupation of the prime minister. History has shown that, aside from our constitutional problems, getting relations right with our neighbour is the biggest political challenge of a Canadian prime minister. He cannot delegate his relationship with the most powerful single player in the U.S. system. There is no better way—sometimes no other way—to engage the president than through personal relations. No Canadian leader recognized the truth of this more than Brian Mulroney, whose hands-on diplomacy delivered agreements on free trade, acid rain, and Arctic sovereignty.

Second, Canada-U.S. relations must also be the constant preoccupation of the Canadian foreign minister. Surprisingly, the effort to master the intricacies of the U.S. political system has not been a priority of most Canadian foreign ministers; they have relegated these issues to the second tier. An exception was Alan MacEachen, foreign minister in the last Trudeau Cabinet, who was responsible for the innovative practice of conducting intensive quarterly meetings with his counterpart, George Shultz.

Third, there must be vigorous central supervision and control in Ottawa. This can only be exercised by the prime minister in Cabinet. Only in this manner can priorities be determined and damaging or marginal initiatives stopped. It is difficult to believe there was a firm hand at the controls when Sheila Copps, the heritage minister, initiated legislation on split-run advertising and excluded the Americans from a conference of cultural ministers in Ottawa, which she convened to consult on how to limit U.S. cultural influence. To snub your neighbours even as you try to cut deals is a disastrous strategy.

Fourth, Canada must be ready to explore arrangements and mechanisms for addressing disputes with the U.S. It is remarkable that there have been so few. As the smaller power, this is certainly not to our advantage. In the past, various mechanisms have been created and disappeared—for example, joint Cabinet committee meetings. Some have not been effective, but others have, such as the NAFTA panels, the International Joint Commission and foreign ministers' quarterly sessions. Also important was the agreement to conduct annual official visits of the president and prime minister to our respective capitals.

Formal arrangements ensure that the more powerful partner focuses on issues of the other. Moreover, they can gear up powerful bureaucratic engines for this purpose. By binding the U.S. to consultative arrangements, we can reduce the number of surprises, and by creating binding dispute mechanisms, we can reduce arbitrariness in the political process of both countries. When there were encouraging reports that Lloyd Axworthy, then foreign affairs minister, was examining ways to achieve a better conflict-resolution process and a new high-level forum to address disputes, the challenge was to convince the U.S. to agree.

Fifth, Canada should deploy a "multiplicity of instruments" in our dealings with the U.S. at the federal and state levels. The complexity of the U.S. political system, the power of individual legislators and the vast array of political players should encourage us to deploy as many channels into the U.S. system as possible, including ministers, parliamentarians, provincial leaders, business executives, senior officials, lobbyists, and others. Canadian influence cannot be too widely spread.

However, it is essential that all aspects of our relationship come within the purview and supervision of the embassy in Washington. While there is, as I have said, great merit in the role of non-governmental and various other players, public and private, commercial and not-for-profit, there are risks associated with any weaknesses in the capacity to steer, advise, warn, establish priorities, relate issues to each other and, above all, manage the relationship. It is an unavoidable fact that various private groups and lobbyists, as well as political sub-units, even government agencies, can work against each other at times, or against the interests of a particular region or industry in Canada—even, at times, against the national interest itself. The federal government and its embassy, acting for the state, is, and must remain, the primary actor in our relations with the U.S., as indeed in all our bilateral relationships.

In the U.S. in particular, absent effective direction, coordination and continuous political assessment, there is a real risk of triangulation by particular interests and their congressional patrons and supporters, as they play off differences between the Canadian players or conflicts in their positions. In the absence of an effective primary player, there is an equal risk of damage to our greater interests at the expense of special interests or those of lesser priority.

The role of "new players" in a "new diplomacy" has become increasingly topical at a time of increasing commercial and cultural globalization and massive increase in trade flows and international concern for human security and human rights. In this context, Professor Stein has issued a stern warning to "traditional realists." "These are people" she writes, "who are accustomed to the monopoly of the state in global politics and the pre-eminence of national security on the foreign-policy agenda." In her view, they "may be uncomfortable with the new players, the new diplomacy, the wide range of assets that are required to assert influence in a densely connected world and broader, more demanding agendas. They had better adjust."

Let me confess to being a traditional diplomat and maybe even—horror of horrors—a "traditional realist" in foreign policy. But this does not lead me to dispute the emergence of "the new diplomacy": the growing importance of new ways to influence the international agenda and the growing role of new partners and players. Professor Stein cites, in particular, non-governmental bodies, multinational corporations (acting as "ambassadors" and promoting "increasingly visible Canadian brands"), new partnerships, alliances with the private sector and not-for-profit societies to advance a human security agenda. This leads Professor Stein to conclude that states and the diplomats who represent them may become only "the first among equals," as citizens, corporations, and non-governmental organizations "participate directly in the new diplomatic formation."

As illustrations, Professor Stein cites alliances between governments and NGOs in developing the Land Mine Treaty and the Statute for an International Criminal Court. She could find further support in the meeting of trade ministers in Seattle, where many non-governmental players (such as the U.S. labour unions) helped to delay the launch of a new round of multilateral trade negotiations.

I fully agree with Professor Stein about the importance of "new players" in "the new diplomacy." As Canadian ambassador to Washington, I strongly advocated public diplomacy, so as to engage new players. In particular, I argued the need for a "multiplicity of instruments" in our relationship with the U.S. I argued that the more Canadian players there were and the more they got involved in the U.S. scene, the more they could represent Canadian views to a multiplicity of players in the U.S. and the more they might be able to form alliances with commercial and political players in the U.S. domestic arena, where so many damaging initiatives arise aimed at Canada's interests.

But for the reasons I have discussed, there are considerable risks involved in the conduct of "the new diplomacy" if, as Professor Stein seems to suggest, the role of the state and its diplomatic representation is downgraded to that of *primus inter pares*.

To consider states as "first among equals" on the international stage is, I believe, to conflate the forces that influence the policies of the actors on the stage with the actors themselves. It is incontestable that the phenomena of well-financed, well-organized, major-league activist groups continue to grow. But the phenomena themselves are not new. Special interests, lobbies, ethnic groups, business associations, farmers, fishermen, protectionists, broadbased environmentalist bodies, multinational corporations, well-organized and well-heeled groups of every kind have long had a deep and sometimes decisive impact on the international positions of governments. This holds true for the governments of superpowers, great powers, and middle and small ones, provided only that they are genuine democracies. As for Canada, think of our fish war with the European Union (we are still paying for this one), our cultural wars with the U.S., our former wine wars with France, and our current dairy wars with everyone. The influencers influence; that is what they do. Governments, for their part, cooperate, bend, yield, reject, act, or fail to act. That is what they do. It is the states, not private groups, that are the primary actors on the world stage and will be so for a long time to come. No new paradigm here.

Important as they are, the role of non-governmental organizations will always be second compared with the role of the democratic state, because these "civil-society organizations," as they are sometimes called, are not accountable to the citizens of a state in the same way as are its elected representatives. Far from it. The methods by which such bodies choose their leaders or spokesmen are not open to the same degree of scrutiny. Churchgoers, dues-payers, financial contributors, members of organizations may be the notional source of the general mandates of these groups. But if their decision-making processes cannot be scrutinized publicly, then in what way are these leaders accountable?

Even if accountability were not an issue for such organizations, the fact remains that they generally advocate a single-interest position or cause, which, no matter how desirable it is in their view, might put them at loggerheads with the general interest, as defined by elected representatives whose power is constitutionally sanctioned. The roles such organizations may play can be of very great value or may sometimes be harmful, but that does not mean that they should be seen as equal actors with states in "the new diplomatic formation." International corporations also exercise great influence in international affairs. But these also do not operate on the same plane as states. Managers of multinational corporations act on behalf of their shareholders, who are increasingly likely to be located in many different countries. What then is the corporation's obligation to those in its home state, or the various host states in which it operates? Most genuinely international corporations are reluctant to fly any single national flag because to do so would make them increasingly alien in other states. Perhaps there are cases where corporations can act as Canadian "ambassadors" and where they can visibly brand themselves as Canadian, but these would surely be exceptional. I know from personal experience that when attempts were made to encourage Canadian international corporations to place their offices in the historic Canadian Embassy in Washington (after the government moved out), there were no takers.

There is, however, one powerful new player on the world stage that is the equal of states, but it is not a private body. It is the supranational organization. At the global level, the World Trade Organization has the direct power to affect international outcomes that would have been impossible to predict a half-century ago. The European Union is, without doubt, a new entrant into the international system of astonishing importance. Nations voluntarily pooling their sovereignty may not be restricted to the greater European region. Similar processes, long-term in nature, are at work in Asia and the western hemisphere. Canada, the U.S., and Mexico have submitted part of their sovereignty to a new institution, the NAFTA panels, which can remand trade decisions of national tribunals. This makes them, in a specific context, a supranational actor on the international stage.

Perhaps the most important of all contributors to the new diplomacy are the media. They will rarely be actors on the international stage, although that sometimes can happen. But when television flashes images across the screen, or the press zeroes in on an issue, they may have far more influence than any other player at the time. The actual power to act or to intervene in a humanitarian war or to negotiate with terrorists, to bargain, embargo, use force, create new rules or whatever, will remain largely the exclusive domain of states. But it is the voice of public opinion that, more than any other factor, shapes and determines foreign policy in a democratic society. Among nongovernment and private players, the media are, alas, more than a first among equals.

POSTSCRIPT BY
JANICE GROSS STEIN

UNLESS THERE ARE MAJOR SHOCKS to the system, Canadians will be living in an ever more tightly connected world in the next century. In this world, Canada will need more than well-trained diplomats and international lawyers. The traditional state-to-state diplomacy that has dominated this century will be only one of several ways that Canada will make its voice heard. Increasingly, the government of Canada will conduct a full orchestra of Canadian players who will participate directly in global politics.

For better and for worse, the twentieth century was the golden age of the state. But as the century closed, the state was losing its monopoly as new players entered the global field. Even the overwhelmingly powerful United States, the unchallenged leader in both military power and cultural dominance, can accomplish far less alone than it would like. It, too, often finds the world frustrating.

After a lull in the mid-twentieth century, processes of globalization are intensifying again, connecting economies and societies in dense networks across and around state borders. Globalization blurs the distinction between domestic and foreign policy, weakening the neat divide between the two envelopes. As economies and societies become more connected, the state is involuntarily retreating from its position of unchallenged control of the economic and political space within its territorial boundaries, with profound implications for the social contract with its citizens, for accountable governance, for configurations of political identity and for its control of the foreign-policy agenda. Indeed, it is increasingly difficult to disentangle foreign from domestic issues and local from global politics.

Canada, like other states, may lose its pre-eminence as the principal focus of political identity and become one among many, bidding for the loyalty of its members in a competitive global marketplace. And, while the Canadian state will certainly retain the authoritative voice in foreign policy, it will have less and less control over an expanding menu of issues. More and more, it will share leadership with new partners at home, who are themselves directly connected to partners abroad.

In the wake of globalization, control, although not authority, has moved up, down and out from the state. It has migrated up to a thickening network of international institutions, some newly created and others newly strengthened. It has also leaked out to non-governmental organizations, multinational corporations and international associations that work effectively outside, across, and through state borders. The reach of the state is being redefined in the face of global forces, and large areas of policy are no longer primarily within its control. As the reach of government has contracted, and the "democratic deficit" over policy has grown, local organizations, newly vibrant, often transparent, and directly accountable to their communities, are increasingly empowered. In federal countries, where state sovereignty is constitutionally divided, sub-national governments are faring better in the changing landscape than central governments.

Traditional realists, accustomed to the monopoly of the state in global politics and the pre-eminence of national security on the foreign-policy agenda, may be uncomfortable with the new players, the new diplomacy and the wide range of assets that are required to exert influence in a densely connected world, and with broader, more demanding agendas. They had better adjust.

The importance of the new array of players is nowhere more important—and more visible—than in our relationship with the United States. The overwhelming importance of the United States to the economic well-being of Canadians is beyond dispute. Although growth in trade with the United States is stagnant, and Canadians have become much more active in Asia than they were even a year ago, the sheer volume of our economic transactions with the United States makes this market central to Canada.

The United States, however, is itself becoming more enmeshed in the global economy. Americans are trading and investing more beyond their borders, their large corporations have a global reach, and the culture they produce is seen and heard around the world. The United States is a global power, but it needs the globe to flourish.

For the foreseeable future, the U.S. will exercise disproportionate influence in establishing the rules of the international economic game as it uses its economic muscle to try to make others adjust to its needs. As a result, we will need to invest extraordinary effort in persuading the president, Congress, even state capitals to recognize not only Canadian needs but also Canada's importance to the American market.

Traditional state-to-state diplomacy will be vital, but it alone is not enough to underscore the importance of the Canadian market to the United States. The increasingly visible Canadian corporate "brand" in New York, Los Angeles, Seattle, and Miami helps to boost awareness of Canada's entertainment, educational, software, pharmaceutical, and telecommunications sectors in the American market. In an ever more tightly connected world, Canadian corporations are ambassadors, not only in the United States, but also wherever they go. And ambassadorships, as seasoned diplomats well know, bring both opportunity and obligation. Canadians working, investing, producing and performing outside Canada are carriers of the brand that grows recognition of Canada beyond our borders.

Nowhere is the widening agenda and the broader range of players more relevant than on cultural issues, now squarely on the broadened Canadian-American agenda. Globalization works to transcend, and even, at times, to supersede national cultures. Its processes create a common cultural environment where everyone who is "connected" has access to the same messages, the same icons and the same calligraphy, produced and disseminated through the tightly controlled transnational corporate networks of television, film, and the "new media." Many of these networks are currently headquartered in the United States and their products increasingly dominate global cultural markets.

Paradoxically, these products no more reflect the diversity of American culture than they do the diversity of others' cultures. Themed fantasy parks, built by large multinationals in the surrounds of urban centres around the globe, are pulling consumers in and away from their "local" cultures. Almost everywhere, culture is becoming deterritorialized, detached from the community and commodified in the global marketplace. Canada, uniquely positioned close to the centre of global cultural production, with many of its citizens sharing a common language with the producers, faces an especially difficult challenge to its "national" cultures.

The revolution in information technologies, which now permits active communication in "real time" and the creation of virtual space, with shared icons and common discourses across cultures and societies, facilitates and accentuates the globalization of culture. It also promotes particularization, differentiation and, at times, increased attachment to local cultures. The multi-channel universe and magazines and music tailored to niche markets accentuate particular differences and local specialization. The "customization of cultural product," so characteristic generically of global economic product, allows individuals and communities to meet their specific needs, without going through the state, in ways that would have been impossible even two decades ago.

As culture homogenizes above the state and fragments below, cultural boundaries—historically an essential component of national identity—are beginning to diverge even more than economic boundaries from national political spaces. The "national" is being systematically weakened as the primary reference category for identity.

These new technologies of information and communication have also enabled actual and virtual groups to define and empower themselves to engage directly on issues of global public policy. Canadian non-governmental organizations are important direct participants in global politics as they reach across state borders to forge alliances. The rapid expansion and decentralization of information systems and the sharp reduction in the costs of international communication have made it easier for non-governmental organizations to build effective partnerships. The resulting pooling of ideas and influence has put them in a much better position to work not only with each other but also with national governments and international organizations.

There are no more vivid illustrations of the capacity of NGOs to organize across state boundaries than their coordinated lobbying, largely through the Internet, against the Multilateral Agreement on Investment, and their concerted opposition to the agenda of the World Trade Organization in Seattle. Canada had an official delegation at the meeting, led by the minister of trade, but outside, on the street and officially accredited to the meeting, were a panoply of Canadian not-for-profit organizations, working with their counterparts from everywhere to shape the global agenda on trade and investment. In the past, NGOs would have lobbied the government in Ottawa, but then would have depended on its officials to represent their interests abroad. Today, the federal voice is still authoritative, but it is only one among provincial, municipal, private, and not-for-profit voices from Canada making themselves heard directly in the global public arena.

Canadian NGOs are everywhere, active across the range of global public-policy issues. In preparation for the summit of the Americas that was to be held in Canada in 2000, they partnered with their counterparts throughout the Americas to advance common agendas. NGOs pooled resources to provide free legal support to state delegations lacking the information and resources to participate effectively in the debate on the statute that created the new International Criminal Court.

NGOs also work with the Canadian government to lobby international institutions. Indeed, Canada's government has taken the lead globally in partnering with the not-for-profit sector. Early on, it worked with the International Committee to Ban Land Mines (ICBL) to promote a global treaty to ban anti-personnel land mines. This partnership of state and non-governmental organizations succeeded where each alone would likely have failed. Similarly, Canada worked closely with the non-governmental sector to develop a statute for an International Criminal Court.

These new partnerships that are at the heart of the "new diplomacy" extend beyond public and not-for-profit collaboration. Long-standing partnering between government and business is expanding and redefining the role of the state, as it strategically invests to promote trade, investment and "branding." Indeed, on the core issue of security, long the defining monopoly of the state, Canada, like many others, is reaching out to new partners.

Canada has turned to the private sector to provide aircrafts to train NATO pilots in its airspace. It has contracted a private company to train police forces on missions it has undertaken with the United Nations. It has contracted with Canadian NGOs to provide support for verification missions it has agreed to provide to international organizations. And it is working more closely than ever before with humanitarian NGOs to help to secure the delivery of humanitarian assistance to war-torn societies.

These partnerships are often exploratory, with unclear rules and a messy division of labour. More and more, however, our government is setting the rules of the game with a broad range of partners and pooling resources from the private and not-for-profit sectors to accomplish shared purposes and expand what Canada can do.

These kinds of partnerships, between states and players from other sectors joined together by shared objectives, are likely to become more and more important in the global politics of the next century. States, and the diplomats who represent them, will become *primus inter pares* as citizens, corporations, and nongovernmental organizations participate directly in the new diplomatic formations.

Canada is well positioned to lead in this new diplomacy. Our experience as a federal society has prepared our political leaders and officials to orchestrate and coordinate. We already have a rich and diverse civil society, with a history of engagement on domestic issues. It is a short and natural step for our non-governmental and private sectors to engage beyond our increasingly porous borders.

These processes are being helped by a Canadian public that is diverse in origin, internationalist in outlook, and unusually well connected across borders. Canada's largest cities increasingly mirror the globe's diverse population. This diversity is Canada's most significant asset in the new diplomacy of the twenty-first century. To use this asset wisely and well will be Canada's most significant policy challenge.

Amid the cacophony of sounds, our conductors will have to choose from a very broad repertoire the music that best mirrors our history, our talents and our values in order to plan a program that has integrity and coherence. They will have to coordinate players at home and abroad, make certain that the players bring the best possible instruments to the concert and then lead the orchestra. Uniquely accountable to the public, as Ambassador Gotlieb rightly argues, the Canadian government alone holds the baton. But, we differ on how the baton should be used. Canadian policy will only be effective if it is well orchestrated and the conductor pays careful attention to all the players, drawing the best from each.

Orchestration of policy in this century will be far more challenging than dictation of policy was in the last, but if the conductors get it right, Canadians—and others—will listen to the concert. They may not always like the music, but they will respect the performance.

HOW DO WE BUILD THRIVING ABORIGINAL COMMUNITIES IN THE TWENTY-FIRST CENTURY?

Will the twenty-first century mean new opportunities for the aboriginal peoples of Canada—or more competing demands for attention?

THE SIX RULES OF SUCCESS

BY TOM FLANAGAN

THE WORDING OF THE QUESTION misconceives the issue. If "aboriginal" includes status Indians, non-status Indians, and Métis, most aboriginal people live in metropolitan areas such as Edmonton, Winnipeg, Toronto and Montreal, as well as in many cities and small towns across the country. They don't live in aboriginal communities, they live in Canadian communities.

People thrive in Canada as individuals and families. There is no mystery about the road to success; it can be summarized in six rules: Go to school and graduate. Get a job and stick with it till you find a better one. Get married and stay married. Have children and invest in their future. Don't acquire a criminal record. Don't drink too much, use illegal drugs, or gamble excessively. Anyone who follows these Six Rules of Success cannot help but thrive in Canada.

The rules are not absolutely inflexible. Some successful people are divorced, or never married, or childless, or alcoholics, or high-school dropouts. But all of the Six Rules are correlated with success, and anyone who violates several of them is headed for trouble.

Canada is one of the world's best places to live. Thanks to the British tradition of constitutionalism and parliamentary government, we enjoy a robust economy, a democratic political system that recognizes civil liberties, and a peaceful society sheltered by the rule of law. High-quality education is generally available—free at the primary and secondary levels, relatively inexpensive at the post-secondary level. Racial prejudice, once a serious barrier to minorities, is no longer a factor; indeed, employment equity programs require many employers and educational institutions to give preference to people of colour, including aboriginal people.

People from all over the world would love to live in Canada. We accept over two hundred thousand immigrants annually; and even though they often have handicaps such as imperfect knowledge of English and credentials that aren't recognized in Canada, most of them thrive because they follow the Six Rules of Success.

The good news for aboriginal people is that those who follow the Six Rules of Success are also prospering. More and more Indians and Métis are graduating from high school, college, and university and finding rewarding careers in business, the trades and professions, and the arts. A substantial Native middle class is growing up across Canada.

Unfortunately, however, the larger picture is still mixed. School dropout rates for aboriginal students are higher than for any other ethnic group. Rates of unemployment, welfare dependency, criminal conviction, and substance abuse remain high, while the rate of legal marriage is lower than for other Canadians. The aboriginal birth rate is the highest in the country, which is a good thing in itself, but will turn out badly for many children who grow up without fathers and are not encouraged to pursue education and paid employment.

In a society such as modern Canada, individuals and families make their own lives, one decision at a time, correcting mistakes and learning from experience. Government has little to do with it, except for enforcing the rules of conduct that preserve freedom of choice, and offering essential public services. By and large, government does that in Canada, creating an open society in which individual success is possible for those who follow the Six Rules of Success. The doors to success in Canada are open; one has only to walk through them.

That is the general picture, but there is one exception of great importance to aboriginal people: the reserves on which about four hundred thousand status Indians still live. There are some fortunate exceptions, but many reserves offer a terrible environment for people to advance their lives.

The fundamental problem of the reserves is the lack of distinction between the public sector and private rights. Unlike the case in other levels of Canadian government, a reserve government is not just a rule enforcer and service provider. In a parody of state communism, it is the effective owner of the land and natural resources of the reserve, the major employer, and the sole landlord. Communism didn't work in the Soviet Union, and it isn't working on Canadian Indian reserves.

Indians did not create this situation. It was created for them by Canadian legislation, motivated by a tragic misunderstanding of Native traditions and a mistaken belief that Indians had no sense of private property. But the reserve system, although intended to be temporary, has endured so long that many Indians have come to believe in the truth of its premise that private property and commerce are alien to their culture.

A better insight into aboriginal culture comes from the name "Ottawa," given to the capital of Canada. The city is named after the Ottawa Indians, whose very name (Algonquin root *adawe*) means "trade." All human beings will be traders and property owners—if the political system gives them a chance.

Ironically, Indians, as the largest landlords in Canada apart from the Crown, are potentially wealthy. The land and resources set aside in the form of reserves would be worth countless billions of dollars if the value could be unlocked. Some entrepreneurial bands are doing that now, but it is a painfully slow process because of the defective structure of property rights.

Most reserves will remain economic backwaters until a way is found to put ownership of their land and resources into the hands of the people who live there. The present arrangement of de facto control by the band council, subject to ministerial approval, is scarcely better than the older arrangement of direct control by the Department of Indian Affairs. Whether local or national, it is still public ownership and political control, when what is needed is private ownership and individual control.

Embryonic forms of private property, including the establishment of customary rights, certificates of possession, and leases, exist on many reserves. But customary rights cannot be enforced in the courts, certificates of possession cannot be sold outside the band, and leases suffer from insecurity surrounding their renewal. The challenge for contemporary statesmanship is to develop existing rights further, so that all Indian people, not just their governing elites, have the same opportunities to succeed and thrive as do other Canadians.

FOUR REQUIREMENTS

BY JEAN TEILLET

IN ORDER TO THRIVE IN THE twenty-first century, aboriginal
peoples require four things. The first requirement is collective
recognition as peoples. Peoples, tribes, nations, communities,
bands, groups, cultures, collectives, societies—the exact label is
not as important as understanding that that the quest is not about
individuals thriving. The quest is to ensure that aboriginal peoples
thrive. This cannot be accomplished by reducing recognition to
individual rights and title. If aboriginal peoples are to thrive,
Canada must recognize, respect, and support their collectives,
their way of life, and the governing institutions that sustain them.

Second, if aboriginal peoples are to thrive, they need adequate
lands and resources. Thousands of years of aboriginal history are
woven into the lands and waters we now call Canada. Aboriginal
connections with these lands created deep roots of identification
with place, a connection that began to change incrementally with
the arrival of Europeans. Since then, the aboriginal story is one of
progressive and cumulative dispossession. The story of the dispossession is not unknown. Thousands of books, learned texts, and
journal articles, as well as several commissions of inquiry have
documented this story. It is not past history, because the dispossession is not finished. It continues every day in Canada as majority
interests authorize the allocation of lands and resources for their

benefit—benefits which do not even trickle down to aboriginal peoples. When aboriginal peoples are dispossessed of their lands and resources, their connections with people, spirit, and culture erode. No peoples willingly acquiesce to dispossession and cultural erosion. So it should not surprise us that aboriginal peoples resist dispossession and struggle to maintain their connections with their lands and resources.

It should not surprise us, but it does. As Geoffrey York has noted, most Canadians know the history of the dispossession of aboriginal peoples but do not acknowledge that this dispossession still continues. Most Canadians live with the illusion that we are more than fair to aboriginal peoples. Events such as Oka and Ipperwash are seen as aberrations, and few Canadians comprehend the cumulative effects of this progressive dispossession. For the most part, aboriginal societies and their needs for lands and resources have either been ignored or seen as irreconcilable with the mainstream Canadian economy. Our history is littered with refusals to protect the land-related interests of aboriginal peoples. Yet, if aboriginal peoples are to thrive in the twenty-first century, their need for lands and resources is absolute. Canada is a large and rich country with a relatively small population. Lands and resources are our greatest source of wealth. There is no logical reason why we cannot share with aboriginal peoples at least some of the lands and resources we originally appropriated from them.

Third, the survival of aboriginal peoples requires cultural space, which means respect for aboriginal cultures, languages, and traditions. Canada has rarely respected aboriginal cultures. Instead, it has relied on assimilation. Indeed, centuries of assimilation efforts were justified on a series of Western values—the duty to Christianize, civilize, educate, enfranchise, bring law to aboriginal peoples, bring democracy and capitalism, and lately the duty to computerize—all seen as ways and means of making "them" more like "us." Whether these evangelistic justifications sprang from religious charity or from a more secular moral high ground, the aim has always been the same—assimilation.

It rarely occurs to Canadians that aboriginal peoples might have their own preferred lifestyles and values. That, as outsiders, they might view Canadian society as wealthy but impoverished, healthy but sick, a country with professed moral or religious convictions that is soulless, a state that believes it has inherited the land but is really borrowing it to the detriment of future generations, a society that proclaims itself to have some aspects of a welfare state but is grasping and greedy, and a society with a justice system that has its blind eye fixed inexorably on aboriginal peoples.

The need for cultural space is not, as Thomas Berger has noted, a lament for a lost way of life. It's not about how uncivilized aboriginal cultures need to evolve into Western, democratic, capitalistic societies. It's not about victims or rewriting the past. Canadian society has refused to take aboriginal cultures seriously. Canadian institutions, values, and use of land are seen as the basis of culture. Aboriginal institutions, values, use of land and language are rejected, ignored, or misunderstood. Cultural space is an opportunity for aboriginal peoples to shape their own future out of their own past and an opportunity not to entrench the past, but to build on it.

Finally, the survival of aboriginal peoples requires self-government. Canada has instituted a multitude of aboriginal policies over the past century and a half. Whether benevolently conceived or not, almost all of those policies have proved disastrous. Its takes only one policy as an example—residential schools—to show the devastating effects when Canada imposes its governance, culture, and values on aboriginal peoples. Aboriginal peoples must be able to make their own decisions about their lives and the lives of their children. Self-government is the mechanism to achieve that. Self-government does not mean that aboriginal peoples will set up in sovereignty in opposition to the nation-state of Canada. Self-government offers aboriginal peoples the opportunity to make their own choices about how they will further their own collectives. Canada needs to understand that it is large, liberal, and democratic enough in its own self-governance to include, as partners, the aboriginal peoples of Canada.

How do we meet these four requirements? In 1982, Canadians made a solemn commitment in the new Constitution. We guaranteed the Indian, Inuit, and Métis peoples of Canada that we would "recognize and affirm" their collective aboriginal and treaty rights. The Supreme Court of Canada has said that recognition and affirmation means that Canada and aboriginal peoples must work together toward reconciliation. The four requirements set out above are the basic components of that reconciliation. They must be implemented incrementally through negotiated agreements and honourable Crown actions.

The very idea of collective rights within a western democracy is anathema to many. The idea that our Constitution demands that we protect those collective rights is still resisted by those who believe that the road to success rests squarely on individual rights and freedoms. These are, as Senator Austin said in the debates leading up to 1982, "old and difficult grievances." So it should not surprise us that aboriginal peoples have a strategy that adopts land claims and self-government as a source of cultural identification. It is a strategy for more than mere survival. It is a strategy that Canadians must support in order for aboriginal peoples to thrive into the twenty-first century.

POSTSCRIPT BY
TOM FLANAGAN

BY ACCIDENT OR DESIGN, Jean Teillet's viewpoint on how aboriginal peoples can thrive is diametrically opposed to mine. Let me explain why her appeal for collectivism, despite its eloquence, does not persuade me. I will comment on each of her four main themes: collective recognition as peoples, lands and resources, cultural space, and self-government.

Collective recognition as peoples. Canada is a free country, in which people can claim whatever identity they wish. Indians can call themselves First Nations, and no one will stop them. Teillet, however, has legal recognition in mind, which runs up against the territorial structure of Canadian government. Legally recognized collectivities include Canada as a whole, the provinces and territories, and cities and rural municipalities. Within that framework, religious and linguistic groups may be given specific rights, for example separate schools for Roman Catholics and French-language services for francophones. But there is no legally recognized collectivity of Roman Catholics (except to the extent that the Church is incorporated under Canadian laws) or of francophones. How could it be otherwise, when Catholics and francophones live everywhere in Canada?

The territorial principle is at the root of all liberal democracies. Civil and political rights can be protected only when people are treated as equal individuals within the territorial limits of legal jurisdictions. It is possible to have a polity in which ethnic communities are legally entrenched (the Ottoman Empire comes to mind), but it will be neither liberal nor democratic.

Lands and resources. Adding together the Indian reserves across Canada, the Métis settlements in Alberta, and various kinds of native land rights in the North, aboriginal people already own a vast amount of territory. Some is good agricultural land; some is rich with timber, oil and gas, and minerals; some is valuable for location; and some may not be worth much now but will become more valuable with population growth. Sadly, much of this land is inefficiently managed because of defective property rights. People live in destitution on reserves that, if commercially developed, would generate wealth to make every band member a millionaire. It makes little sense to transfer more Crown land to people who, because of the governmental and legal system imposed upon them, are not equipped to manage the lands they already have.

Fixation on land, moreover, is counterproductive for material progress. Most Canadians are doing fine despite owning no more land than required to locate their family home. Success in a modern economy depends mainly on developing skills and knowledge that other people wish to purchase. Hunting, fishing, and trapping can provide a livelihood for a relatively tiny number of Canadians, aboriginal or otherwise.

Cultural space. As a free society, Canada allows people to nurture whatever culture they wish. All sorts of religious and ethnic groups keep alive their own cultural traditions on Canadian soil. But there are choices to be made. At one extreme, Jewish and Japanese Canadians maintain certain cultural traditions while integrating fully into Canadian society. In fact, their members are so successful that they enjoy the highest average standard of living in the country. At the other extreme, the Hutterites keep themselves out of the mainstream of Canadian society. They maintain their separate identity, but their material standard of living is impoverished. Attachment to a sixteenth-century Low German dialect supports their cultural heritage, but hardly facilitates success in the modern world. Of course, they define success differently. No one objects if they want to live the way they do, as long as they pay their own way (and pay their taxes!). Analogies with the situation of aboriginal people are not hard to draw.

Self-government. As long as there are Indian reserves and Métis settlements, there is a need for self-government for these territorial communities. Most of them resemble rural municipalities, while a few are more like small towns or suburbs. But the institutions of aboriginal self-government badly need to become more transparent and accountable to their own people. The books need to be opened so that reserve members know what is going on. Band elections, like other elections in Canada, should be supervised by an independent monitoring agency. Most importantly, reserves need to start taxing their own residents to pay for at least part of the services they receive. The cry of the American Revolution was "No taxation without representation," but the obverse is equally true: "No representation without taxation." Unless people have to reach into their own pockets to pay for services, democracy is nothing but a conspiracy against the public treasury. Revisions of the *Indian Act* are urgently required, but when the government proposed something sensible along these lines in 2002 (Robert Nault's *First Nations Governance Act*), the Assembly of First Nations went all out to defeat it. I'm not optimistic about reforms in the foreseeable future.

POSTSCRIPT BY
JEAN TEILLET

IT IS INDEED IMPORTANT to recognize that many aboriginal peoples do not live on reserves and that we must address the issues that arise among those who live on reserves and in urban and rural situations. However, it is wrong to treat off-reserve aboriginal people as if they are no longer members of their aboriginal collectives, have lost their aboriginal identity and are assimilated into the non-aboriginal society. Such a notion denies the very existence and persistence of aboriginal cultural identities and societies. It also fails to account for the fact that most aboriginal people never lived on reserves in the first place and that many of our cities, for example Winnipeg and Sault Ste. Marie, grew up around pre-existing aboriginal villages and trading centres.

The claim that all aboriginal people need do to thrive is follow simple "rules for success" is an assimilation argument—and not a subtle one at that. It is simply an advertisement for the Canadian dream. Simplistic reiterations of these rules have not been persuasive with aboriginal people to date. They are unlikely to become suddenly successful on repeat performances.

In order to understand any failed advertising campaign, one must look first to the product on offer, then to the consumers, and finally to the price. The product offered is success or the Canadian dream. The consumer is aboriginal people and the price is giving up aboriginal identity. Why are most aboriginal people not thriving? Why don't they buy the Canadian dream? The answer is simple—they don't like the product they see and the price is too high. What are the solutions? Since the consumers remain the same, either we must modify the product, lower the price, or both.

If we want aboriginal people to buy into the Canadian dream, we must understand what we have offered them to date. After all, the Canadian dream success story is not a new product. It has been on offer for over three hundred years. To date, success has been advertised as Christianity, civilization, education, jobs, and money. The reality has been forced relocations, lost children, lost lands, imposed religion, residential schools, over-representation in our jails, high disease and suicide rates, alcohol, drugs, and poverty. To say the least, it is not a pretty picture. Small wonder that simply restating the rules of success to be followed upon purchasing this product are not persuasive. Aboriginal peoples are not generally happy consumers and have not found success with the product they have been forced to consume or the price they have had to pay.

Let us examine just one aspect of the product on offer: "private ownership and individual control of reserve lands." This is the introduction of a marketplace for reserve lands and the suggestion that the public ownership of reserve lands combined with political control by the band is the problem. In reality, it is the quantity and quality of the land that is the problem, not the collective nature of the title or the entity that controls the land base. Most reserves are too small to allow any economic development at all. Indeed, we can see that, in the few situations where there are sufficient resources and lands of good quality, aboriginal peoples can derive good economies and healthy societies. Making reserve land alienable would have only one result: the ultimate destruction of the collective land base. This particular product is merely a blueprint for dispossession and does not even address a real problem. There is nothing inherently wrong with collectives or collective land holdings. All societies value the collective—whether that is in the form of the family, the community or the nation. Canada currently has myriad complicated land holdings, some of which are collectively held, inalienable and subject to public ownership and political control. Private ownership divorced from public control simply does not apply to all lands in Canada and never has. To suggest therefore that the marketplace is some kind of panacea for the economic problems of reserves because it is the rule that applies to other Canadians is to set out the issues in too simplistic terms. The opening up of reserve lands to the marketplace would simply open them up to what Lord Denning called "the selfish, the thoughtless and the ruthless." This suggestion is disingenuous at worst, unhelpful at best and provides only one solution to impoverished aboriginal economies—assimilation.

Finally, we must honestly look at the high price of success—forfeiture of aboriginal identity and culture—in order to participate in the Canadian dream. If this price had ever been acceptable to the vast majority of the aboriginal peoples of Canada, we would not have any left. Assimilation would have been accomplished. But it has not worked for two reasons. First, because most aboriginal people deeply value their identity and have never considered relinquishing it. Second, because they feel that Canadians don't really want them as they are. They feel that Canada wants them only as an interesting part of history. In other words, Canadians are inordinately fond of the fact that we used to have aboriginal people but are much more uncomfortable with the fact that we still have them. The rules for success are merely old ways and means towards a final solution that would accomplish that preference.

IS MULTICULTURALISM AN ASSET OR A LIABILITY IN A POST-9/11 WORLD?

Since the events of 9/11, issues of multiculturalism have received even more attention than usual—and increased tension is sometimes the result. As a proudly multicultural country, will Canada find that its policies or its role internationally will be affected?

MULTICULT REVISITED

BY GEORGE JONAS

I DO NOT OPPOSE IMMIGRATION. I came to Canada from Hungary fifty years ago. For me to oppose immigration would be opposing myself. Closing doors to victims of persecution or poverty is against all my instincts. For old-fashioned liberals of my ilk, freedom of movement, whether of goods or people, is a basic ideal. I know immigration can benefit the host country under the right circumstances, but as a former refugee, I'd extend asylum to people at risk even if the circumstances were wrong.

I do oppose multiculturalism. It's not because I have any problem with ethnic or cultural diversity. On the contrary, I take a civilized society's acceptance of diversity for granted. I don't care where people are coming from; I care about where they are going. The problem is that under multiculturalism many people are going to where they've been coming from—in which case they might as well have stayed where they were.

What's good about multiculturalism is in no way predicated on it. The fair and equal treatment of individuals regardless of race or ancestry, combined with respect for their customs and values, including the most outlandish ones—as long as they don't conflict with the law of the land—is fine, but it's also a given in a decent, Western-style democracy. Being tolerant requires conversion to multiculturalism no more than being charitable requires conversion to Christianity.

I do not oppose being kind to strangers. Being kind to strangers is my stock in trade. I oppose being unkind to Canada. I oppose respecting every heritage except this country's. I oppose treating Canada as if it were Grand Central Station. Or a public bath. Or, indeed, a public urinal.

As a social policy, multiculturalism has not so much backfired in Canada as led to its predictable consequences. It awarded citizenship to aliens, alienated citizens, and turned two grand solitudes into several petty ones. These results, intended or not, flowed from what seemed like an intriguing social experiment in the 1960s to Pierre Elliott Trudeau and his merry band of sorcerer's apprentices. As newly empowered politicians, inspired and validated by the spirit of their times, they set out to alter this country's ethnocultural makeup, along with its institutions and ethos. Their three-step program for revamping Canada culturally and demographically entailed: a) reducing immigration from "traditional" (read: West European) sources; b) increasing it from non-traditional sources; and finally c) shifting from Conservative prime minister John Diefenbaker's ideal society of unhyphenated Canadians to the Trudeaucratic Liberal ideal of a multicultural Canada.

Multiculturalism was said to build on an earlier Canadian tradition, the so-called cultural mosaic. In contrast to the American "melting pot," with its implied pressures of assimilation, the cultural mosaic had the appearance of a more tasteful and restrained model of nationhood. In reality, the notion of a mosaic had less to do with good taste than with British (and French) standoffishness. Canada's founding nations were reluctant to be thrown into a pot with the riff-raff of the world to be melted. The hint of apartheid built into the concept of a "mosaic" was there to ensure the dominant position of the English and the French.

Multiculturalism aimed for the very opposite: to do away, not just with the British and French, but the First World character of Canada as a nation. Trudeau's ambitious, unannounced, possibly unexamined and merely intuitive design would, within two or three generations, take Canada out of the ambit of Christendom altogether and establish it as an advance pawn of the Third World in the western hemisphere. As an incidental—or perhaps not so incidental—benefit, multiculturalism was also expected to drown the noise of Quebec's demands for cultural distinction in the din of other cultures clamouring for the same acknowledgement.

One result of the multicultural model was a retreat from the principle that immigration should serve the interests of the host country first. The host country came to be viewed less and less as a nation, a legitimate entity with its own culture, and more and more as a political framework for various coexisting cultures. Newcomers were encouraged not to regard themselves as immigrants seeking to fit, but as explorers, if not conquistadores, whose quest was to carve out a congenial niche in Canada for their own tribes, languages, customs, or religions.

I do *not* suggest that Trudeau and his acolytes wished or expected their policies to contribute to alienation, dissension, and terror in the world. Canada's pirouetting *bon vivant* leader neither desired nor envisaged the twenty-first century being ushered in by disaffected Muslims shooting Dutch politicians, crashing airliners into Manhattan skyscrapers, blowing themselves up in London buses and Madrid trains, and—allegedly—plotting to behead Canadian prime ministers. Chances are that, stumbling about in a mixture of psychoactive fumes and what Tom Wolfe called a "quasi-Marxist fog," Trudeau's crowd came to believe that the ills of the planet were due to Western ways, and the sooner they could replace the crumbling edifice with a sixties-type New Left Utopia, the better. If they had no real blueprint for it, it didn't matter: blueprints were for fuddy-duddies, linear thinkers, not for the free spirits of the spontaneous generation.

In the climate of the times, it was politically incorrect to note that all nations have themes, characters, narratives, myths, and organizing principles, and any attempt to limit a cultural leitmotif within a country, well meaning as it may be, has the capacity of turning a nation into a railway station in which passengers mingle, occasionally sharing a destination, but no destiny. Multiculturalism would have made some sense if it had been designed to turn a country from a peaceable kingdom into an array of hostile, inward-looking xenoliths. Since it was designed to do the opposite, it made none.

Intellectual fashions rise like tides. They easily overwhelm scholarship, logic, and common sense, at least in the short run. In a climate of nouvelle cuisine, serving a dish of raw and separate ingredients may sound like a good idea. I suggest it is a recipe for indigestion, if not food poisoning. A nation is not a tossed salad but a hearty soup, and it's prepared in a pot. A melting pot, if you will. Better make it a cauldron.

SCAPEGOATING MULTICULTURALISM

BY HAROON SIDDIQUI

CANADA HAS HISTORICALLY BEEN multicultural, but constitutionally so only since the 1982 Charter and legislatively so since the
1988 *Multiculturalism Act*. Therefore the question—is multiculturalism an asset or a liability in a post-9/11 world?—is as valid or as
redundant as it was before September 11, 2001.

During the First and Second world wars, Ukrainian, Italian and
Japanese Canadians were deemed a security risk and interned, for
varying periods. Ottawa has since apologized for those decisions
and, in the case of Japanese Canadians, paid hefty reparations.

During the 1919 Winnipeg General Strike, many Russian,
Ukrainian, and Jewish Canadians were suspected of being
Bolsheviks plotting a revolution.

During the Second World War, German Canadians, fearful of
being deemed a "fifth column" for the Nazis, hid their racial-
ethnic identity, so much so that their population count went down
in the national census.

During the 1970s and 1980s, Irish Canadians were suspected of
secretly funding the terrorist Irish Republican Army. Some may
well have, as the Irish Americans most certainly did.

In the decades following the establishment of Israel in 1948,
Jewish Canadians were at times accused of dual loyalty.

Now we are suspicious of Muslim Canadians.

An old pattern can be said to be repeating itself.

The counter-argument would be that, unlike the other suspected minorities of an earlier era, some Muslim Canadians not only harbour an extraterritorial loyalty to the *ummah* (the global community of Muslims), but would, in its name, resort to violence, either because they are motivated by the Islamic ideology of "jihad" (holy war, in popular parlance) or because they want to exact vengeance for the killing of tens of thousands of Muslims in Iraq and Afghanistan, and/or for the Israeli occupation and oppression of Palestinians.

In support of this line of thinking, one would cite first 9/11 itself, carried out by foreigners who had infiltrated the United States; second, the homegrown terrorist bombings of Madrid and London, carried out by people who were born or bred in Spain and England; and third, the case of eighteen Toronto-area youths charged in the summer of 2006 with terrorism-related charges.

Even if one were to concede the point—that militant Muslims constitute a dangerous category all their own, the like of which we have never witnessed in our history—the security risk they might pose to Canada has little or nothing to do with multiculturalism.

The United States is decidedly not multicultural, insisting on melting everyone's identity into an "American" one. Spain could be said to be anti-multicultural, in that it tolerates much discrimination against its one million Muslims. Britain is not officially multicultural, though it has made half-hearted attempts at accommodating different ethnic, cultural, and religious groups. Only Canada is proudly multicultural. Yet none of this has made any difference to the terrorists. Or if it did, it did so for the better, since Canada has not been hit, as of this writing, in the post-9/11 wave of terrorism.

Similarly, the 1985 bombing of an Air India jet, allegedly by Canadian-based Sikh militants, and also the financing of the terrorist Tamil Tigers in Sri Lanka by Tamil Canadians during the 1990s could not credibly be said to be the products of the "permissive" policies of multiculturalism. It is widely believed that the Air India tragedy, the biggest terrorist act in Canadian history, could have been avoided and, at the very least, its perpetrators brought to justice, had the Royal Canadian Mounted Police and the Canadian Security Intelligence Service had been more competent. That incompetence had nothing to do with any mistaken desire on the part of the Mounties or CSIS agents to be, somehow, "nice" to an ethnic minority. Equally, multiculturalism did not stop Ottawa from eventually outlawing Canadian funding for the Tamil Tigers. If, as has been argued in some quarters, the governments of Jean Chrétien and Paul Martin took too long to come to that decision, their dithering was not a function of multicultural sensitivities, as sometimes suggested, but rather of a reluctance to move against a Liberal vote bank—a routine, albeit not laudable, political imperative. Why is catering to an "ethnic" vote bloc any worse than, say, bowing to the farm lobby or to the dictates of Bay Street?

In the post-9/11 period, Ottawa did not in any way feel hobbled by multicultural sensitivities to implementing a slew of draconian legislative and administrative initiatives. It toughened up the *Immigration Act*, tightened the *Access to Information Act*, gutted the *Privacy Act*, and passed two sweeping pieces of legislation, the *Anti-Terrorism Act* and the companion *Public Safety Act*. It created a super-ministry, the Department of Public Safety and Emergency Preparedness, as Canada's answer to the Bush administration's authoritarian bureaucratic behemoth, the Department of Homeland Security. All this was done over the stern objections of not just Arab-Muslim Canadians but also the federal Privacy

Commissioner, the Information Commissioner, the Canadian Human Rights Commission, the Canadian Bar Association, the Canadian Civil Liberties Association, the Canadian Newspaper Association, and several other groups.

When Auditor General Sheila Fraser later found some of the $7.7-billion anti-terrorism measures wanting, she singled out the ineptitude of various departments and officials, not any real or imagined multicultural hurdles they may have encountered. When the RCMP public complaints commissioner Shirley Heafey went to court to force the Mounties to divulge the information she needed to probe complaints by some Canadian minorities against alleged RCMP heavy-handedness, she criticized the Mounties for their excessive secrecy, not their sensitivity to any multicultural political correctness. And while there have been some complaints that the spies working for the RCMP, and CSIS as well as the Communications Security Establishment (the agency that intercepts phone calls, etc.) feel constrained by the Charter, the suggestion was dismissed by the Security Intelligence Review Committee, the civilian oversight body, which came to the totally opposite conclusion: that our spies have too little legislative oversight.

Canada's multicultural imperatives did not prevent the Maher Arar tragedy, or the reported torture of three other Canadian Arabs in Syria, allegedly with Canadian complicity.

Nor did it stop Citizenship and Immigration Canada in 2003 from labelling twenty-three Muslim men of Pakistani and Indian origins as suspected terrorists, allegedly part of an al Qaeda sleeper cell, whose cited suspicious activities included being seen near the CN Tower and taking pictures in the vicinity of the Pickering nuclear plant. (Eventually, not a single terrorism-related charge was proceeded with, and the young men, illegal immigrants all, were deported or they "voluntarily" left, their lives ruined.)

Multiculturalism did not stop the Canadian authorities from detaining, for prolonged periods and without charge, five long-time Canadian residents of Arab origins under the so-called security certificates on secret evidence. Whatever the merit or otherwise of this procedure, the relevant point here is that multi-culturalism did not impede Ottawa's dogged implementation of this policy in the name of national security.

Conclusion: whereas both multiculturalism and the Charter of Rights continue to enjoy broad public support, a vocal minority has never fully accepted either. It can always be counted on to dredge up either or both as scapegoats for any real and imagined ills of Canada, such as the proposition, heard throughout our history, that the country is going to the dogs by letting in the wrong sorts of immigrants.

POSTSCRIPT BY
GEORGE JONAS

CANADA HAS BEEN ETHNICALLY diverse for much of its history but, as Haroon Siddiqui accurately observes, it has been legislatively and constitutionally multicultural for only twenty-five years or so. We've had much experience with diversity and little with multiculturalism.

Diversity probably benefited Canada. Can multiculturalism hurt it? I suggest it can.

The immigrant societies of the New World were aware from the outset that sentiments of kinship, tribal nostalgia, and what George Washington called in his farewell address "the illusion of an imaginary common interest" between the nations of newcomers' ancestry and their new country of citizenship, could lead to divided loyalties. The best way to counter this tendency was felt to be integration and, to the extent possible, assimilation.

Before the question of multiculturalism was ever raised, the U.S. "melting pot" was an answer to it. So was the similar notion of the "unhyphenated Canadian." Both worked. The loyalty of "new" Canadians and Americans was remarkable. During two world wars, although Canada and the U.S. treated German, Italian and Japanese immigrants and their descendants with shabby suspicion, as a rule they responded with unfailing patriotism. For every "Tokyo Rose" (the American GIS' nickname for Ikuko Toguri, a Japanese-American woman, born in Los Angeles, who broadcast Japanese propaganda during the war) there were thousands of Japanese-American soldiers who gave their lives to fight fascism.

The pattern continued during the Cold War among former nationals of hostile communist countries who found refuge in North America. These newcomers of varied ethnicity and religion, from Eastern Europe to Vietnam, were as supportive of the values and interests of their adopted countries as native-born citizens of Western descent, if not more so. Few Americans opposed the anti-American antics of Fidel Castro as resolutely as Florida's ex-Cuban community.

It was only in the last thirty years that a new type of immigrant emerged: the immigrant of dubious loyalty. This was followed, even more alarmingly, by the disloyal native-born, sometimes of immigrant ancestry, sometimes of Islamic conversion.

The new immigrant seemed ready to share the West's wealth but not its values. In many ways, he resembled an invader more than a settler or a refugee. Instead of making efforts to assimilate, he demanded changes in the host country's culture. He called on society to accommodate his linguistic or religious requirements.

Some demands were fairly innocuous: in 1985, a Sikh CNR railway worker refused to exchange his turban for a regulation hard hat. In 1991, less innocuously, a newly appointed Toronto police board commissioner of Asian extraction declined to take the traditional oath to the Queen.

The host societies' usual response was accommodation. In Canada, turbans were substituted for hard hats; the language of the police oath was changed. We allowed ceremonial daggers in schools. But accommodation only escalated demands. Requests for cultural exemption were soon followed by openly voiced sentiments of disloyalty. By the late 1990s, a Muslim group in Britain saw fit to express the view that no British Muslim has any obligation to British law when it conflicts with the law of Allah.

Disturbing as such talk was, it wasn't unlawful. Dissent was within our democratic tradition. Unfortunately, the new dissenters weren't democrats. Their "dissent" culminated in threats, fatwas, assassinations, and finally massacres in American and European cities.

How did this come about? Three reasons stand out:

1. I mentioned this before, but will repeat it for emphasis. We retreated from the principle that immigration should serve the interests of the host country first. Instead of welcoming diversity, we started worshipping it. We forgot that, when groups of distant cultural and political traditions arrive in significant numbers, they're likely to establish their own communities, not merely as colourful expressions of ethnic tapestry—festivals or restaurants—but as separate cultural-political entities.

2. Next, we tried to turn this liability into an asset by promoting multiculturalism. We began flirting with the notion that host countries aren't legitimate entities with their own cultures, only political frameworks for various co-existing cultures.

3. Finally, in militant Islam, we've come up against a culture for which the very concept of rendering to Caesar what is Caesar's and to God what is God's is alien. Fundamentalist Islam considers that everything belongs to God (or rather, some mullah's idea of God). This concept doesn't envisage citizenship commanding as high a loyalty as faith.

"An old pattern can be said to be repeating itself," Siddiqui observes. We used to be suspicious of German, Italian, and Japanese Canadians, and now we are suspicious of Muslim Canadians. My colleague is right. We tend to be suspicious of ethnic or religious groups whose members bomb or plot against us, whether at Pearl Harbor or in London, Madrid, Toronto, New York. He seems to find this surprising. I don't.

Refugees from Islam are no threat. Neither are Islamic settlers. Islamist colonizers are. That's where current immigration trends and multiculturalism become a volatile mix. Extending our values to others is one thing, but modifying our values to suit others is a vastly different proposition. Immigrants don't threaten national identity. Colonizers do. The political scientist Samuel Huntington notes that Latin American newcomers seem to be creating a "demographic '*reconquista*' of areas Americans took from Mexico by force in the 1830s and 1840s." Groups undigested sit like lumps in a nation's stomach. After they reach critical numbers, they may no longer be assimilable.

Siddiqui concludes that "both multiculturalism and the Charter of Rights continue to enjoy broad public support." I rather doubt if multiculturalism does, but in any event, internment of Japanese Canadians enjoyed public support, too, during the war. Broad public support doesn't make a dim policy bright.

Multiculturalism makes it difficult to safeguard Canada's identity against immigrants whose goal is to carve out a niche for their own tribe or religion in what we no longer view as a country but a tabula rasa, a civilizational vacuum, an empty space. When Canada is no longer regarded as a culture with its own narratives, but a clean slate for anyone to write on, immigrants of the new school will be ready with their own texts, including some that are not very pleasant. The sound you hear (as I wrote in 2002) is the sharpening of their chisels.

POSTSCRIPT BY
HAROON SIDDIQUI

GEORGE JONAS HAS MADE some central points, to which I feel the need to respond.

"Under multiculturalism, many people are going where they've been coming from—in which case they might as well have stayed where they were."

This argument predates multiculturalism, and, in fact, is as old as Canada. Immigrants have always been accused of harking back to their homelands. Many did, most particularly the English and the French.

They should have stayed home, eh?

Multicultural practices are fine so long as "they don't conflict with the law of the land."

They don't. Where does it say that multiculturalism is a licence to break the law? Neither Section 27 of the Charter (Trudeau's doing) nor the *Multiculturalism Act* (passed by the Mulroney Tories) exempts anyone from the laws that apply equally to all citizens.

The law, for example, does not allow polygamy, even if some Muslims may dream of it and many members of the fundamentalist Church of Jesus Christ of Latter-Day Saints have practised it for decades. That the RCMP has been tardy in going after this Christian sect has nothing to do with multiculturalism.

"I oppose treating Canada as if it were Grand Central Station."

Statistics do not support the proposition that immigrants are passing through Canada on the way to someplace else. An overwhelming majority stay. Some move on, mostly to the United States, or back to where they came from, such as Hong Kong, because of lack of employment or business opportunities commensurate with their skills.

Historically, some naturalized Canadians have also retired to their native lands, such as Great Britain, Italy, and Greece.

Multiculturalism awarded citizenship to "aliens, alienated citizens, and turned two grand solitudes into several petty ones."

By definition, "aliens" are the people to whom an immigrant nation grants citizenship, after they have lived on the right side of the law for a prescribed period. As for solitudes, we have had plenty of them through our history. For example, the Poles lived on the wrong side of the tracks for generations, as did the Jews in their "ethnic ghetto" in North Winnipeg.

Pierre Elliott Trudeau and his ilk "set out to alter this country's ethnocultural makeup...[by] reducing immigration from 'traditional' (read: Western European) sources; increasing it from non-traditional sources, and finally shifting from Conservative Prime Minister John Diefenbaker's ideal society of unhyphenated Canadians."

In fact, what Trudeau et al. did was to end racist immigration policies. That created a level playing field for potential immigrants, from anywhere. And while Dief made grand speeches, Canadians remained happily tethered to their hyphens— Ukrainian-Canadians, German-Canadians, Jewish-Canadians, Italian-Canadians, etc.

"Canada's founding nations were reluctant to be thrown into a pot with the riff-raff of the world to be melted. The hint of apartheid built into the concept of a 'mosaic' was there to ensure the dominant position of the English and the French. Multiculturalism aimed for the very opposite...take Canada out of the ambit of Christendom altogether and establish it as an advanced pawn of the Third World in the Western Hemisphere."

I like this formulation because it gets at Jonas's confusion and his chief complaint: the English and the French instituted Apartheid Lite—not a good thing, obviously, in that they treated, say, the Hungarians as riff-raff—but multiculturalism committed a greater sin, that of letting in the heathens, non-white ones at that.

Similar sentiments were expressed at various times in our history about the Jews, the Japanese, the Chinese...

Multiculturalism made us "retreat from the principle that immigration should serve the interests of the host country first."

It hasn't. We invite immigrants not for altruistic reasons but because we need them (see federal, provincial, and business projections regarding looming skills and labour shortages).

Trudeau and other multiculturalists may not have envisaged "disaffected Muslims shooting Dutch politicians, crashing airliners into Manhattan skyscrapers, blowing themselves up in London buses and Madrid trains."

Holland, Spain, and Britain are not officially multicultural, nor is the United States. But that made no difference to the terrorists, the same way that other legal and cultural niceties made no difference to the IRA or the Basque separatists.

It has become "politically incorrect to note that all nations have themes, characters, narratives, myths, and organizing principles."

Multicultural Canada does have a theme, a narrative, and several organizing principles—to start with, that no one group can dominate others, that all peoples (even non-Christians and non-whites) are equal, and that all citizens must adhere to the rule of law, including the Charter of Rights and Freedoms, our common holy parchment.

Multiculturalism is "a recipe for indigestion, if not food poisoning. A nation is not a tossed salad but a hearty soup."

On the contrary, it is a recipe, first, for much food for thought and, second, for the best foods of the world, not merely roast beef, poutine, and goulash.

As for tossed salad, I like it as a metaphor for multicultural Canada, in the same way that Laurier liked to think of Canada as a Gothic cathedral: "I want the marble to remain the marble, the granite to remain the granite, the oak to remain the oak—and out of all these elements I would build a nation great among the nations of the world."

His dream is a reality today.

ABOUT THE CONTRIBUTORS

NEIL BISSOONDATH

Neil Bissoondath is a renowned novelist and familiar cultural commentator. His book, *Selling Illusions: The Cult of Multiculturalism in Canada*, was a national bestseller. His novel *The Worlds Within Her* was shortlisted for the 1999 Governor General's Award for fiction.

BARRY COOPER

Barry Cooper is a professor of political science at the University of Calgary. He is the author of numerous books on political philosophy and Canadian public policy, including *The Klein Achievement*.

TOM FLANAGAN

Tom Flanagan is a professor of political science at the University of Calgary. His book *First Nations? Second Thoughts* (2000) received an award from the Canadian Political Science Association for the best book of the year on Canadian politics. He has been an expert witness for the Crown in important native-rights cases such as Blais, Benoit, Chief Victor Buffalo, and Manitoba Métis Federation.

ALLAN GOTLIEB

Allan Gotlieb had a distinguished career in the foreign services, including acting as Canada's ambassador to Washington from 1981 to 1989. He is currently senior adviser to the law firm Bennett Jones LLP.

JACK L. GRANATSTEIN

Jack L. Granatstein taught at York University from 1966 to 1996, and is now the distinguished research professor of history emeritus. He was the director and CEO of the Canadian War Museum from 1998 to 2001, and driving force behind the building of its new home. He has written more than fifty books on Canadian history, including the bestselling *Who Killed Canadian History?*

CHARLOTTE GRAY

Charlotte Gray is the author of six award-winning non-fiction bestsellers, including biographies of Alexander Graham Bell, Susanna Moodie, and E. Pauline Johnson. An adjunct research professor at Carleton University, she is the winner of the Pierre Berton Award for popularizing Canadian history, and was the celebrity advocate of Sir John A. Macdonald on the CBC's *Greatest Canadians*.

MICHAEL IGNATIEFF

Michael Ignatieff is an historian and award-winning author of fiction and non-fiction works, including *Scar Tissue*, which was nominated for the 1993 Booker Prize. He is the member of Parliament for Etobicoke–Lakeshore, and in 2006, was a candidate for the leadership of the Liberal Party of Canada.

GEORGE JONAS

George Jonas is the author of fourteen books, including the international bestsellers *Vengeance* and *By Persons Unknown* (with Barbara Amiel). His critically acclaimed novel, *Final Decree*, has appeared in five editions. Currently, he writes two weekly columns, one for the *National Post* and another in syndication for CanWest News Service. His columns and articles have appeared in the *National Review*, the *Chicago Sun-Times*, the *Daily Telegraph*, and the *Wall Street Journal*, and have been collected and published as books. His latest books are *Beethoven's Mask* (memoirs, 2005) and *Reflections on Islam* (essays, 2007).

NAOMI KLEIN
Naomi Klein is a columnist with the *Globe and Mail* and a regular television commentator on social issues. Her first book, *No Logo: Taking Aim at the Brand Bullies*, was a national bestseller.

GUY LAFOREST
Guy Laforest is the director of the department of political science at the Université Laval and the author of numerous publications on Canadian political theory and intellectual history, including *Trudeau and the End of a Canadian Dream*.

OVIDE MERCREDI
Ovide Mercredi is an aboriginal politician and peace activist, who has specialized in constitutional law, and who became a chief strategist for the Assembly of First Nations during the Meech Lake Accord discussions. From 1991 to 1997, he served as the national chief of the Assembly of First Nations.

PETER C. NEWMAN
Peter C. Newman is one of Canada's leading authors, with more than nineteen award-winning books to his credit. He is also senior contributing editor at *Maclean's* and a columnist for the *National Post*.

BOB RAE

Bob Rae is a partner at the Canadian international law firm Goodman, Phillips and Vineberg. He served as the twenty-first premier of Ontario from 1990 to 1995, and is the author of two books, *From Protest to Power* and *Three Questions: Prosperity and the Public Good*. In 2006, he was a candidate for the leadership of the Liberal Party of Canada.

HAROON SIDDIQUI

Haroon Siddiqui is editorial-page editor emeritus and columnist for the *Toronto Star*. He has been the *Star's* national editor, news editor and foreign affairs analyst, and covered, among other seminal events, the Soviet invasion of Afghanistan, the Iranian revolution, the Iran-Iraq war, and lately, the emergence of India as an economic and geopolitical power. He is the author of *Being Muslim*, an account of post-9/11 politics.

JANICE GROSS STEIN

Janice Gross Stein is the Belzberg Professor of Conflict Management in the department of political science at the University of Toronto and a fellow of the Royal Society. In 2006, she received the Order of Canada. Professor Stein is director of the Munk Centre for International Studies at the University of Toronto and a regular television commentator on foreign-policy issues.

JEAN TEILLET

Jean Teillet is a partner in the law firm of Pape Salter Teillet. She practises primarily in the field of aboriginal rights law with a particular emphasis on Métis rights law and has acted as counsel for aboriginal groups in several Supreme Court of Canada aboriginal rights cases. She is also involved in negotiations of modern land-claims agreements for First Nations. Her publications include *Exoneration for Louis Riel: Mercy, Justice or Political Expediency?* and the annually updated *Métis Law Summary*. She is the great-grandniece of Louis Riel.